COUNTY COLLEGE OF MORRIS

D0290131

THE FETAL POSITION

THE FETAL
POSITION

A RATIONAL APPROACH

TO THE

ABORTION ISSUE

CHRIS MEYERS

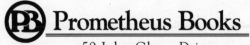
Prometheus Books
59 John Glenn Drive
Amherst, New York 14228-2119

Published 2010 by Prometheus Books

The Fetal Position: A Rational Approach to the Abortion Issue. Copyright © 2010 by Chris Meyers. All rights reserved. No part of this publication may be reproduced, stored in a retrieval system, or transmitted in any form or by any means, digital, electronic, mechanical, photocopying, recording, or otherwise, or conveyed via the Internet or a Web site without prior written permission of the publisher, except in the case of brief quotations embodied in critical articles and reviews.

Inquiries should be addressed to
Prometheus Books
59 John Glenn Drive
Amherst, New York 14228–2119
VOICE: 716–691–0133
FAX: 716–691–0137
WWW.PROMETHEUSBOOKS.COM

14 13 12 11 10   5 4 3 2 1

Library of Congress Cataloging-in-Publication Data

Meyers, Chris, 1968–
    The fetal position : a rational approach to the abortion debate / by Chris Meyers.
        p. ; cm.
    Includes bibliographical references and index.
    ISBN 978–1–59102–768–3 (pbk.)
    1. Abotion—Moral and ethical aspects. I. Title.
    [DNLM: 1. Abortion, Induced—ethics. 2. Beginning of Human Life—ethics.
3. Philosophy, Medical. 4. Public Opinion. HQ 767 .15 M612f 2010]

HQ767.15.M49 2010
179.7'6—dc22

                                                                2010006838

Printed in the United States of America

CONTENTS

PREFACE

Abortion is a very difficult moral problem. There are many activists, however, on both the pro-life and the pro-choice side of the issue who would have you believe that abortion is a very simple moral problem. They talk as if it is *obvious* that abortion is morally wrong or as if it is *obvious* that a woman has every right to have an abortion. If this book accomplishes nothing else, it should prove that the morality of abortion is not at all obvious, that it is indeed a vastly complicated problem.

I am a philosopher by trade. We philosophers love difficult problems. The scholarly literature on the morality of abortion could fill the Superdome to its rafters. I would like to pretend that I have read every important philosophical writing on the morality of abortion, but I have not. And even if I had, it would take a dozen books to summarize it all (a dozen very tedious and boring books). What I hope to do in this short book is to provide a philosophical analysis of some of the most common arguments offered by non-philosophers for and against abortion and to introduce the reader to the main philosophical arguments on both sides of the issue. We cannot cover every argument, nor can we completely analyze the arguments that we do cover. But I hope that whatever philosophical analysis that I can offer will serve as an example of how to engage in critical thinking about moral issues. Once people acquire some skill in careful reasoning, they can go on to think through the issues themselves. I do not intend, in this book, to tell anyone what to think, but rather only to *show* people *how* to think.

Part 1 of this book explains what philosophy is and how it can allow us to reasonably resolve moral issues, or at least try to. This account of the philosophical method is then applied to two competing worldviews: the religious pro-life view with its belief in a soul and the secular pro-choice view with its more scientific conception of human life. The struggle between these two worldviews is not taken very seriously among academic philosophers today, at least not in the English-speaking world. But still, good philosophy can help to determine which view of life is more reasonable. Those who do not find this debate compelling could skip chapters 2 through 4 and move on to part 2.

Part 2 deals with several types of arguments on both the pro-life and pro-choice side of the debate. Most of these arguments come in several versions— some cruder versions appealed to by activists, and then some more sophisticated and esoteric versions offered up by professional philosophers. It is not essential to read chapters 5 through 9 in the order that they are presented in the book. Besides discussing the virtue approach to moral issues like abortion, chapter 10 contains something of a conclusion, although I expect my readers to think for themselves and draw their own conclusions in the end.

ACKNOWLEDGMENTS

I t is customary, in the acknowledgments section of a book, for the author to express gratitude for some scholarship or grant that allowed her the free time to work on her project. For me, there was no such scholarship or grant. Instead, a hurricane named Katrina swept through the southern Mississippi town where I live, shutting down power for weeks and blocking every road with several fallen trees. With nothing to do and nowhere to go, I began to write this book. School was canceled for two weeks. There was no television, no telephone service, and no radio. All the businesses were closed. I started writing at night by candlelight between meals of cold canned beans and warm canned beer. That initial start provided enough momentum to write the entire thing. But although Katrina did provide me with the idle hands needed to start work on my project, I feel no sense of gratitude to the storm that destroyed my beloved New Orleans.

There are several people who helped make this book better. Any deficiency in this work is entirely due to the author's shortcomings and occurred only in spite of the helpful comments of friends and colleagues. First of all, I would like to thank Eileen Papazian, who first inspired me, many years ago, to realize the importance of the abortion issue. I would also like to thank my mentor, Tom Carson, who gave me useful feedback on an abortion paper that I managed to publish before I had even thought of writing a book on the issue. (That paper informs much of chapter 7 of this work.) My colleague Sam Bruton provided very critical comments on the first few chapters, which (I hope) helped me keep the book balanced and fair to both sides. I am also thankful to my cat Tigger, who kept me company during most of the writing, usually curled up in my lap. (May he rest in peace.) Most of all, I am thankful to Natacha Vacroux, who read multiple drafts of the entire book. Her comments greatly improved the quality of writing of the finished product, and I never would have finished without her encouragement.

INTRODUCTION

FANATICS

One evening, several months ago, I was at a local pub here in southern Mississippi enjoying a few beers while writing chapter 5 of this very book. (Yes, I wrote some of this book while drinking beer.) There were some local townsfolk playing pool near my table who were intrigued by the sight of someone writing in a bar. One of them finally approached and asked me what I was writing. My gut instinct told me to say something to make him go away. "Tell him it is a textbook on accounting," I thought to myself, "or a business report on the rising cost of coffee beans."

But my conscience urged me otherwise, not so much because of the moral presumption against lying but because I worried that my inclination to lie was motivated by a cynical or even condescending attitude. Was I being a snob? Did I see these men as ignorant backwater yokels incapable of appreciating my book project? I decided to give this man the benefit of the doubt. I was hopeful that he would prove my gut instincts wrong, especially since the book was intended for ordinary people rather than professional scholars.

So after a brief pause I told him, "I am working on a book on the morality of abortion."

"Well, are you fer it? Or agin' it?" he asked in a tone that made it pretty clear that he was very much agin' it.

"Well," I tried to explain, "that's not really what the book is about. I am trying to analyze the arguments of ordinary—"

11

"Are you fer it . . . or *agin'* it?!" he demanded again, even more pointedly this time. He was not interested in the book or the arguments or the truth, and he made it pretty clear that I had better not be *fer* it.

I tried to defuse his hostility by pointing out that no one is going to be *for* abortions; no one would think that we should try to have *more* of them. To him this was hairsplitting. This man did not want to hear any double-talk from some Yankee intellectual. He seemed shocked that I would even consider the possibility that we should allow people to have abortions under any circumstances. After receiving a stern lecture implying that I was some sort of baby-killing monster, I decided to work on my book in peace at home, and to be a little more discreet about my project in the future.

This unwillingness to consider the arguments on both sides of the issue is not unique to the pro-lifers. Fanatics can be found on both sides of the debate. I am sure that I might have received the same kind of reaction from someone on the pro-choice side had I been in a more politically liberal environment. If I were back at the coffee shop near my alma mater in Chicago, I might have gotten the same hostile questioning, this time implying that I had better not be opposed to the right to terminate one's pregnancy. Unless I were to give immediate and unequivocal affirmation of the pro-choice line, I might have received a different but equally stern lecture, this time implying that I was some sort of woman-hating caveman.

THE PROBLEM: IDEOLOGY FIRST

With many moral and political issues—especially emotionally charged ones with potentially high stakes and opportunistic politicians fanning the flames of rhetoric—people typically decide *first* which side they are on, and only afterward do they choose the reasons supporting their view. They decide first that abortion is wrong and then look at the issue with their minds already made up. Or they decide first that every woman has a right to an abortion and then sort through the arguments with a biased eye.

This, it seems obvious to me, is putting the proverbial cart before the proverbial horse. What if scientists were to decide first which theories were true and which false, and only after that to look at the data? We would probably still be living in the dark ages drawing blood to cure illnesses and trying to turn rocks into gold.

The purpose of this book is to look at the arguments first and then to judge the morality of abortion on the basis of the better arguments. The only agenda I have is to promote rational and critical thinking (and to base our beliefs on that thinking). We need to carefully examine the arguments on both sides, especially the arguments given by nonphilosophers, which are often neglected by professional scholars (like me). This will require first presenting these arguments in the fairest and most charitable way. We must be careful to avoid presenting a caricature of the arguments, especially those that support the side we disagree with. Such inaccurate representations of the opposing view can be easy to refute; but such refutations are too easy and do not prove anything.

Next we must carefully analyze the arguments to see if we can find any flaws in them. It is especially important to critically analyze those arguments that we are inclined to agree with. Often arguments that seem very convincing at first will be found to be weak on closer inspection. We must not let our sympathetic tendencies allow us to go too easy on certain arguments.

At this early point in the book, all we need concern ourselves with is being fair and coming down on whichever side is best supported by the evidence. We can decide whether or not abortion is morally wrong (and whether or not it should be legal) only after we carefully examine all the arguments in support of each side, just as a scientist or a historian can decide the truth or falsity of some given theory only after all the available data has been carefully considered from an impartial standpoint.

For these reasons, this book is not written for those who have already made up their minds on the issue—on either side—or for those who are not willing to question whether or not abortion is morally acceptable (though, of course, those people are still welcome to *purchase* the book). It is not written for my pool-playing friend who accosted me at my neighborhood pub, and it is not written for my left-wing feminist pals in my old college neighborhood of North Chicago. In short, fanatics on either side are not likely to find this book tolerable. It is, however, written for those who, like most Americans today, lie somewhere in the middle: those who are sometimes pulled toward the pro-choice side and sometimes toward the pro-life side, those who hold one view but without much conviction, or those who are just plain confused by the whole mess.

Still, even the nonfanatical readers of this book might reasonably want to know where the author stands on the issue—whether I am "fer it or agin' it." Surely if I claim that careful philosophical analysis can show whether or not abortion is morally wrong, then I must favor one side over the other. (Presumably I would favor the side that is better supported by philosophical analysis.) Normally I would feel an obligation to state my position openly in the name of "full disclosure." But in this instance I think that stating my settled judgment on the matter would be very misleading and counterproductive. For I only came to that settled judgment after going through all the thought processes contained in this book (and then some). All the time that I was first mulling over the arguments and counterarguments contained in these pages, I was undecided on the issue. I wavered one way and then the other way, as each argument seemed compelling at first but then fell apart under closer scrutiny. I think it is very important that the readers allow their beliefs to be determined by the arguments and reasons given for each position, not by the author's personal views.

I am a professional philosopher, not an activist. The purpose of this book is not to convince the reader that abortion is wrong or that it is not wrong. The purpose is to show that highly emotional and contentious issues can be considered rationally and to show how to analyze dispassionately the arguments on both sides. I do not intend to do any thinking for the reader but rather aim to show him how to think for himself. If I am an activist, I am not a pro-life or a pro-choice activist; I am a *pro-rationality* activist.

For these reasons I will not say where I personally stand on the issue, not here or even at the end of this book—though maybe by the end it will be obvious which side is supported by better arguments. I intend merely to lay bare all of my analysis of the most common and convincing arguments on both sides. The reader will have to agree or disagree with my analysis, and she will have to decide upon her own conclusion in the end.

BURDEN OF PROOF

In many debates one side has the burden of proof. That means that if neither side can prove its case, victory goes by default to one side over the other. Having the burden of proof means that you must prove your claim to be true; if neither side can prove its case, you lose. This is how burden of proof works in our criminal justice system. The burden is on the state to prove that the accused is guilty. If the defense can prove that the accused is innocent, then so much the better. But if neither side can prove its case convincingly, then the accused must be judged to be not guilty.

The same situation occurs in scientific, historical, and even philosophical debates. Generally the side making the stronger claim has the burden of proof. Suppose, for example, that a believer and an atheist are arguing over the existence of God. In this case neither side has the burden of proof—their burden is equal. This is because both are making equally strong claims. One is arguing that God definitely exists while the other is arguing that God definitely does not exist. If neither side can prove its claim, then the debate ends in a draw.

But if the believer is arguing with an agnostic—one who holds that we don't know whether God exists—then the burden of proof is on the believer. This is because the wishy-washy claim of the agnostic, that God may or may not exist, is much weaker than the claim that God definitely does exist. Thus if the believer cannot provide sufficient proof for the existence of God, then the agnostic wins. (The atheist would also have the burden of proof in a debate with the agnostic, because the claim that God definitely does not exist is much stronger than the claim that we don't know one way or the other.)

Is there a burden of proof in the abortion debate? It may seem that way for this reason. Although we tend to think of moral issues in terms of right (should be done) or wrong (should not be done), the moral status of an action actually falls into one of *three* categories: morally wrong actions, morally right actions, and morally neutral actions (those that are optional; neither right nor wrong). This morning, for example, I had oatmeal for breakfast. That was neither right nor wrong, morally speaking. It is not a moral issue. Whether I have oatmeal or waffles, or if I skip breakfast entirely, does not matter from a moral point of view. I have no duty to have one breakfast or another, and I certainly do not deserve any blame or praise based on what I ate this morning (assuming I was not eating human flesh).

Now, no one on the pro-choice side would say that one has a duty to have an abortion or that someone deserves praise for deciding to have an abortion. Pro-choicers would not say that we should try to promote abortions or that those women who want to carry their healthy fetuses to term should be encouraged to abort instead. According to the pro-choice view, having an abortion is not morally wrong, but it is not morally right either. It is a morally neutral act, at least in most situations.

One could argue that calling an action morally right or morally wrong is to take a stronger position than to claim that it is morally neutral. We need some reasons for thinking that a given act is one that we ought to do and encourage in others or one that we ought to avoid and prevent. Without any reasons for or against some particular kind of action, we must assume that it is merely optional—one that we may do if we wish or may decide not to do if we so prefer. Moral neutrality seems to be the default.

There is a major flaw in this line of reasoning. Let us draw again on the analogy with criminal law: if the prosecution can prove that it is more likely than not (but still not certain) that the accused is guilty, then we must presume he is innocent. This is because it is believed to be better to let a guilty person go free by mistake than to wrongly punish an innocent person. We should err on the side of caution. Now suppose that we could establish that abortion, more likely than not, is wrong; but we are still uncertain. It seems that erring on the side of caution would be to forbid abortions, because it is better to mistakenly forbid something that is not wrong than to allow something that is wrong.

Furthermore, we could recast the debate in terms of whether we should allow abortions. The pro-choice side would surely not claim that banning abortions is morally neutral. Pro-choicers, as the term *choice* implies, make the positive claim that a pregnant person has a right to terminate her pregnancy (at least within certain parameters). They claim that it would be wrong to prevent someone from terminating her pregnancy if she so chooses.

Thus the burden is equal. And this helps us to clarify the positions in the debate. The pro-life side argues that abortion is wrong and for that reason should be banned. The pro-choice side argues that each person has the right to terminate her pregnancy and thus abortions must be allowed. Notice that this allows for an intermediate position. The fact that one is exercising a right does not necessarily mean that one is acting blamelessly. The right to freedom of speech, for example, allows people to say nasty, despicable things. Given that they are exercising their rights, it would be wrong for us to censor them. But that does not mean that they are not doing anything morally wrong.

One could hold that abortion is morally wrong, but that there is still a right to have one. Or one might hold the slightly weaker position that abortion is morally wrong but should not be illegal (without claiming that there is any right to it). We cannot criminalize everything that is morally wrong. Cheating on one's spouse is morally wrong, but I do not think we should put people in jail for doing so (though I would never go so far as to say that one has a *right* to cheat on one's spouse). We should keep in mind the weaker intermediate position, even though we will focus on both the pro-life claim that abortion is seriously wrong enough to warrant criminalization and the pro-choice view that a woman has a right to terminate her pregnancy.

Despite the equal burden of proof on both sides, pro-lifers have typically shouldered most of this burden, and so most of the arguments we will consider are those intending to show that abortion is morally wrong or that it should be banned.

A FEW BASIC ASSUMPTIONS

There are a few claims on which I am going to assume my readers will agree. Though these claims might not gain universal agreement by all rational persons, they are fairly weak claims that most members of modern Western society will accept.

First I am going to assume that there are objective moral truths. Consider the following moral claim: it is wrong to torture babies for pleasure. This is objectively true even though some (fortunately, very few) people might not agree, just as it is objectively true that the earth is round even though some people still believe that it is flat. I assume that anyone who is interested in the morality of abortion accepts the claim that the rightness or wrongness of a particular action (such as performing an abortion) is to be discovered and not merely decided upon.

If there are no objective moral truths, then we are left with two alternatives: moral relativism and moral nihilism. According to moral relativism, an action is wrong if it is disapproved of by some person or group. On this view we do not disapprove of actions because they are wrong; rather, disapproval is what makes an action wrong. If one group disapproves of abortion then it is morally wrong *for that group*. And if a different group approves of abortion (or does not disapprove of it) then it is *not* morally wrong for that group. There are serious problems with this sort of view. But we need not concern ourselves with refuting moral relativism. Anyone who wants to know whether abortion is right or wrong (anyone who would be interested in reading this book) is presumably not merely interested in finding out whether abortion is disapproved of by herself or other people, but whether or not it is wrong. Thus it can be assumed that anyone who has read this far into the book is not a relativist.

Nihilism, on the other hand, is the view that there are no moral truths. Nothing is morally wrong or right and all moral beliefs are false. Morality is a mere fiction. This view is even less plausible than relativism. Nihilism would entail that torture, murder, rape, genocide, and so on are not morally wrong. Anyone who is concerned with moral issues—whether she is a pro-choicer or a pro-lifer—is not going to be a moral nihilist. So we need not deal with those issues in this book.

The next assumption I am going to make is that it is morally wrong, in most cases, to kill an ordinary person like you or me. Of course, there may be extraordinary circumstances such as self-defense. But even some staunch pro-lifers will approve of abortion in extraordinary cases, as, for example, when carrying the fetus full-term will kill the mother. Anyone who does not agree that killing people is usually morally wrong is someone who we are not going to be able to have a reasonable discussion with regarding the morality of abortion.

Next, I am going to assume that normal adult women are *persons* in the same sense, and to the same extent, as are normal adult men. They have the same moral status and possess all of the same moral rights (and obligations). Women are not property or objects to be used and exploited. They are fully capable of making their own decisions (barring some particular mental impairment) and pursuing their own self-chosen projects.

Finally, I am going to assume that there is nothing morally wrong with using contraception such as condoms, birth control pills (including the "morning-after" pill), as well as natural contraceptive means such as withdrawal and the rhythm method. (The IUD may be another matter since it does not prevent conception.) Though some devout Catholics may feel that contraception is wrong, I am going to claim that this is not a moral issue but a special rule for membership in that religious denomination. Thus, using contraception might make you a bad Catholic, but it does not make you a bad *person*. Those who think that contraception of any form is morally wrong are not going to be able to discuss the morality of abortion in a reasonable manner.

Fortunately, there are very few people in our society who hold such extreme views. I have never met anyone who thinks indiscriminate killing is morally OK, or who views women as mere incubators whose sole purpose is birthing babies. Even those who disapprove of the morning-after pill generally do so because they mistakenly confuse it with the RU-486 abortion pill.

WHAT THIS BOOK IS ABOUT

Our question is a moral one. By *moral* I mean that it is a matter of the most stringent reasons for acting (or not acting). It is a matter of how we ought to behave, all things considered. Should we, individually or as a society, try to forcibly prevent people from having abortions? Or does a pregnant woman have a right to terminate her pregnancy (in which case we should let her decide whether or not to carry the fetus full-term)?

We are not concerned with questions about the history of abortion. We are also not concerned with sociological questions about the various attitudes people have toward abortion, in our society or others. Nor are we going to get involved in theological debates about what the Bible (or Koran, or the Vedas, etc.) has to say about it. And we would do best to steer clear of the politics of the pro-life versus pro-choice struggle.

Finally, our question is also not a legal one. This might need some explanation. A legal inquiry into the abortion issue would seek to determine whether abortion *already is* legal or illegal, or whether its legality or illegality can be inferred from other laws. This is what the US Supreme Court attempted to decide in the 1973 *Roe v. Wade* case. Was the Texas law banning abortion consistent with the US Constitution? Pro-lifers typically bemoan the court's decision. But whether or not the Supreme Court made the correct decision is irrelevant to the *moral* issue of abortion. We are not concerned with whether or not abortion is legal but whether it *should be* legal. It would be perfectly consistent for a pro-lifer to agree with the court that the Constitution implies a legal right to terminate one's pregnancy while still maintaining that abortion should be banned (and that the Constitution should be changed, if necessary, to allow the ban).

Part 1 of this book (chapters 1 through 4) looks at a radical disagreement between certain members of the pro-life camp and certain members of the pro-choice camp in terms of their respective worldviews, or at least in terms of their views of what constitutes human life. This fundamental disagreement is an enormous obstacle to reasonable debate. We will use philosophical analysis to provide a neutral ground on which to assess the relative merits of these two views.

Part 2 (chapters 5 through 10), on the other hand, will look at various pro-life and pro-choice arguments that do not revolve around disputed notions of what it means to be alive. These arguments include appeals to the potential of the fetus, the "golden rule," various consequences of abortion policies, and so on.

PART 1

CHAPTER 1
PHILOSOPHY TO THE RESCUE!

P art of the reason, I suspect, that little progress has been made toward reaching any kind of consensus about the morality of abortion is the lack of willingness on the part of those with passionately held opinions to seriously engage in honest debate. Some people, on both sides of the issue, dogmatically assert their views without considering fairly the arguments for the contrary position. These people are only encouraged by certain politicians who pander to their base for support of their political careers.

Perhaps, to be more charitable, some people hold their views dogmatically because they do not realize that it is possible to present evidence for and against moral positions and to use rational thinking to determine the truth of the matter. They can hardly be blamed for being unaware of this kind of critical thinking, for there are so few examples to be found in public discourse today. This is where philosophy can, and I believe must, come to the rescue. It can provide a forum for debating such seemingly intractable issues. This is not to say that we will, in this short book, determine once and for all the correct view to which everyone will immediately agree. But philosophy can provide the means for getting some real discussion started in a fruitful direction.

WHAT IS PHILOSOPHY?

Before addressing exactly how philosophy can assist us in this debate, we should first ask, "What is philosophy?" The answer will enable us to see how philosophy can help us resolve (or at least openly debate) the abortion issue. This question is not an easy one to answer. Many philosophers would even disagree over the correct characterization of what it is they do. This may seem very odd to nonphilosophers, but the difficulty of saying exactly what philosophy is actually serves as an illustration of what philosophers do and what philosophy is about.

In philosophy, everything is open to questioning—even of what philosophy itself is or should be. This is not the case in other fields. In physics, for example, there is virtually unanimous agreement as to what physics is and what physicists should be studying. Physics is the study of the most basic constituents of the physical world—in other words, matter and energy—and the mathematically describable laws governing their interactions in space (or something like that). This definition forms the foundation for all physics and so cannot be questioned, at least not within physics itself. To question whether observation and experimentation are reliable indicators of reality, or whether matter exists independently of our perceiving it, is not to ask scientific questions but *philosophical* questions.

Once, when I was a young college student first studying philosophy, I was having dinner with my then girlfriend's family when her father, who was a physicist, asked me, "What exactly is philosophy anyway?" To my utter embarrassment, I was unable to give any more than the sketchiest of answers. I hemmed and hawed and made some vague and lofty comment about the "search for truth." Of course, that is correct as far as it goes, but it does not go nearly far enough. Philosophy *is* the search for truth, but that is inadequate as a definition. After all, the sciences are also involved with the search for truth, as are history and math. That philosophers seek the truth does not distinguish philosophy from a large number of other academic and scientific pursuits. Yet it is nevertheless an important thing to remember because it does help to distinguish philosophy from literature and poetry, which are concerned more with meaning, rhetoric, and beauty than with truth. (No one criticizes a poem or novel because it depicts things that did not really happen.) Remembering that philosophers are seeking truth might help dispel any misconceptions based on stereotypes of philosophers sitting around thinking "deep thoughts," daydreaming about unknowable things, or pontificating about the meaning of life.

How does philosophy differ from other truth-seeking endeavors? Many areas of inquiry are identifiable not so much by their methods (which they may share with other fields) but by their subject matter. For example, biology is the scientific study of living organisms, and psychology is the study of human behavior. Mathematics studies numbers and their relations, while history studies past human events. There is, however, no particular domain that sets philosophy apart from other fields. We cannot say, "He studies X? Then he must be a philosopher!" Philosophy can be about anything. There is philosophy of science, philosophy of mind, philosophy of history, and so on.

One thing that does distinguish philosophy from other fields is that it asks more fundamental questions, questions that cannot be decided by observation. While physicists study the most basic constituents of matter and energy through experiment and observation, philosophers ask, "What is real?" and "What can we know?" This is the first part of our definition of philosophy: it is critical thinking about the most fundamental questions. How does philosophy of science differ from science? Philosophy of science questions the very foundations of science, asking questions about the meaning of scientific statements as well as the source (and degree of certainty) of scientific understanding. How does philosophy of mind differ from psychology? Psychology studies (among other things) human behavior and mental states such as beliefs and emotions, while philosophy of mind asks what *are* these beliefs and emotions. Are they, for example, physical brain states? Functional dispositions that mediate between perceptual input and behavioral output? Something independent of physical matter?

Another way philosophy differs from other fields of study is in its methods. Observation is the primary method of inquiry in science. The scientist formulates a hypothesis, makes a prediction based on the theory being tested, and then performs a critical experiment, if possible. The most important part is the last part. The scientist must observe the outcome and compare it with the predictions. With some theories, such as physical anthropology, experimenting is not possible. But anthropologists can make predictions and look for evidence to support them. For example, if humans evolved from apes, then we can predict that we should find fossils of apelike protohumans.

Other disciplines besides science look to experience and observation. Although historians do not formulate general theories like scientists do—and they do not necessarily make predictions—the methods of history are, like science, based on observation. Typically historians rely on the observations of others that have been passed down through testimony. They also observe the effects of past civilizations and historical events, such as ruins and artifacts. Historians need some observation, by themselves or others (in the past or present) in order to discover historical truth.

Philosophy has no particular method. Unlike science and history, it relies primarily on rational argumentation alone. In this respect it more closely resembles math than science. Mathematics does not rely on any observation of the world but can be done "in one's head" (or on paper). So the other part of our definition of philosophy is that it is the search for truth *through rational argumentation* rather than observation.

None of this should seem to imply that philosophy is better or more important than science. Philosophy is never going to cure AIDS or solve world hunger or even help make a breakfast cereal that will not get soggy in milk. And anyway, scientists can go about their business just fine without answers to these fundamental questions. The psychologist can discover many important things about human emotion and cognition without worrying about whether or not such states could exist in a computer. Biologists can usefully classify animal and plant species without answering questions about whether these categories are invented or discovered.

Nevertheless, I think that philosophy can be very useful. And its usefulness comes precisely from the fact that it is not committed to any distinct method and is not confined to any specific topic. It can be useful precisely because it *can* be about anything and does not need to rely on some definite set of basic axioms. This is what will make it so helpful in the abortion debate.

INCOMPARABLE WORLDVIEWS

One of the central problems with the abortion debate in both politics and public discourse (or perhaps we should call it the abortion "fight," for rarely is there any real debate) is that the two major sides do not share enough common ground for discussion to take place. On one side we have the religious branch of the pro-life movement led by conservative Catholics and Fundamentalist Christians, and in the other camp we find pro-choice activists who mainly approach the issue from a more secular perspective. There are, of course, other camps that are smaller or less vocal. But these two sides largely define the terms of the debate today. Unfortunately, they start with such radically different fundamental principles, and so radically disagree in their basic commitments and overall worldviews, that they cannot communicate with each other. It is as if they are not even talking about the same thing or using the same language.

The widely divergent starting points make discussion on the issue impossible—even for those who want to discuss the issue fairly and open-mindedly. When the two sides do try to talk, they end up talking past each other, each one bringing up points that the other regards as irrelevant. For meaningful and productive dialogue to happen there must be some way for the two parties to find common ground. By analogy, suppose the parents of high school students are discussing the quality of one of the school's coaches. Some of the parents think that the job of a high school coach is to win games, while others think that the job of a coach is to develop skills and teach good sportsmanship. The coach might easily be a success according to one set of criteria and yet a failure according to the other standards. In order for the parents to have a meaningful dialogue, they will first have to have a discussion about what constitutes good coaching at the high school level.

I believe that what often happens with the abortion debate is that the two biggest camps—the religious pro-lifers and the more secular pro-choicers—disagree not only on the morality of abortion but also on much more fundamental issues, such as what constitutes human life and what properties a being must have to warrant moral consideration. One of these groups, on the pro-life side, consists of people with a predominately religious outlook who believe that each living human being has a soul and that it is this that makes a person worthy of moral consideration. The other group, on the pro-choice side, consists of people with a decidedly less religious view who tend to see the world, including human life, more from the perspective of the natural sciences. They see the human being primarily (though not necessarily exclusively) as a biological organism and believe that human beings warrant moral consideration because of some more-or-less observable property, such as self-consciousness, the ability to feel pleasure and pain, or the capacity for rational thought.

Of course, these two groups are not the only ones. Many people with an opinion on the matter do not fall into either camp. There are devout Christians who reject the claim that God forbids abortion and who believe in a woman's right to terminate her pregnancy. (There is even a political organization called Catholics for a Free Choice.) There are also some who have a decidedly naturalistic worldview and yet believe that it is wrong to kill a fetus, not because it has a soul but for other reasons. Nevertheless, the two major groups—the religious pro-lifers and the more secular pro-choicers—dominate the debate, and the profound differences in their respective worldviews is a serious obstacle to reasonable discussion.

ARTICLES OF FAITH

Let's start with those in the religious camp who adhere to what we will call the *sanctity of life* principle. People with this outlook are committed to certain articles of faith. By "articles of faith" I mean something distinct from, and more specific than, fundamental beliefs. To believe something "on faith" is to believe it without evidence. When Doubting Thomas demands concrete evidence of the crucifixion and resurrection, Jesus says to him, "Oh ye of little faith!" Thomas lacks faith because he is not willing to believe without evidence. Articles of faith are basic, fundamental beliefs that are not proven and are believed despite the lack of any evidence or proof. Typically this is because they *cannot* be proven; there can be no evidence for them or against them. Since these fundamental articles of faith are not accepted because of any preponderance of evidence, believers tend to hold these beliefs dogmatically and are often not willing to question them. This is not necessarily a character flaw given that often, just as there is no evidence for these beliefs, there is also no contrary evidence against them.

I am not criticizing articles of faith. For one thing, our thinking about ultimate questions of what is real or true, or what is valuable, must start somewhere. You cannot begin construction of a building without a foundation, and once it is built you cannot go around making changes to the foundation. Furthermore, as we shall soon see, articles of faith are hardly unique to religious views but are at the core of virtually every systematic picture of the world. The secular-thinking people on the pro-choice side are as wedded to their own articles of faith as are the religious pro-lifers. Secular thinkers may be even more dogmatic at times because they are not aware of how their beliefs are grounded on faith.

RELIGIOUS PRO-LIFE AND THE SANCTITY OF LIFE

What are the core beliefs that serve as articles of faith for adherents of the religious pro-life position? We must be careful not to over-generalize about members of this group, or worse, to offer up a caricature. I will try to provide a sketch of the fundamental claims of this view that its adherents will find acceptable. First of all, there is a commitment to the existence of a God, usually thought of as an omniscient, omnipotent, and benevolent creator of the universe.

Essential to this religious sanctity of life principle is the existence of a soul—some supernatural element partly constituting the human being and human life. This soul is conceived of as a nonphysical, spiritual entity—though for rhetorical purposes, religious pro-life advocates often instead speak of the fetus as having a "Life" (with a capital *L*) in order to avoid being dismissed by more secular-minded people. We need to sift through the rhetoric to get at the arguments, so I say we call a spade a spade and use the term "soul." This soul is believed to be the source of human life and is what makes human life demanding of profound respect.

The notion of a soul is what makes this a religious outlook. But what leads to the sanctity of life principle is the further claim that all living human beings have a soul at every moment while they are alive. On this Judeo-Christian notion of the soul, only human beings have a soul. This raises them above nonhuman animals. The sanctity of life principle is a moral prohibition against killing anything with a soul. Since any human being that is alive has a soul, the sanctity of life principle forbids the terminating of any human life from the moment of conception up until there is no sign of life of any kind (until the human being "gives up the ghost," as it were). Even someone like Terri Schiavo (brain-dead but still biologically alive) has a soul. And according to this view, it would be wrong to end that life intentionally.

SECULAR PRO-CHOICE AND THE NATURALIST VIEW OF LIFE

Those in the other main camp—the majority of those who defend the right to an abortion—have a more scientific view of the world and see the human being primarily (though not necessarily exclusively) as a biological organism. They have on their side all the support of a well-worked-out, empirical, scientific theory of biology. Nevertheless, it is important to understand that this more naturalistic view also has its articles of faith. This is something that many, especially those who hold this view, fail to recognize. Those with a more scientific worldview are often blind to the fact that, although the particular claims made within the sciences are well supported by empirical evidence, *adopting* a scientific worldview is not itself—nor can it be—supported by any empirical scientific evidence. That would be circular reasoning: appealing to observation to show that we should believe only what we observe. Science itself has as a foundation certain basic commitments that are merely assumed to be true and that cannot be proven (at least not scientifically).

What are the articles of faith for the naturalists? For them, what makes something human and what makes a human being alive must be some set of observable physical properties or processes. Being human, on this view, means having a certain genetic makeup and physiology. Being alive is simply the occurrence of certain biological processes such as growth, reproduction and cell division, nutrition, and so on. There does not seem to be anything of great moral significance in any of these physiological processes themselves, and I suspect that both sides would agree with that. After all, these biological processes can be found even in plants, and few people on either side would be willing to grant moral rights to plants. (Even vegans have to eat something.)

For this reason, both sides look elsewhere for what it is that gives human beings special moral status, for what it is that gives us obligations to our fellow humans that we do not have to rocks or trees or even nonhuman animals. For the religious sanctity of life camp, this special status is granted to us by the possession of a soul. The secular pro-choicers, on the other hand, insist that we must find this moral status in something observable, so they point to certain psychological faculties such as self-consciousness, rationality, sentience, and so on (or the potential for these).

This is where it becomes apparent that the naturalist's position rests, at least in part, upon faith. For the naturalist, explanations of anything observable must always themselves also be couched exclusively in terms of observable phenomena. The naturalist need not be an atheist and need not believe that everything that exists is physical. It may be that humans have a soul and that this soul is a nonphysical spiritual entity. But this soul cannot be what makes us tick biologically, since being biologically alive is a physical property and something that we can observe. We can observe whether or not someone is biologically alive by testing her pulse, seeing if she is breathing, and so on. So whatever explains being biologically alive must itself be observable. For the naturalist this is probably going to be observable physiological processes, such as heartbeat, breathing, digestion, cell division, and so on, all of which can be reduced to chemical reactions.

Regarding life, the naturalist will likely say that there is no evidence for the existence of the soul and thus it is the religious view that rests on mere faith. But this is not fair, for by *evidence* the naturalist is assuming that only scientific, observable evidence can count in favor of the existence of something. This belief, that empirical evidence is the only legitimate kind of evidence, is the article of faith upon which the naturalist bases his view. In criticizing the sanctity of life adherents for relying on mere faith, the naturalist is taking his *own* articles of faith and unfairly demanding that his religiously minded opponents fight on his naturalistic terms. The religious pro-lifers should reply that there may be other evidence for the soul, evidence besides empirical scientific observation.

Likewise, if the believers in the supernatural soul turn to scripture for their evidence, then their case is very weak. Divine revelation would be very good evidence for a belief or system of beliefs—assuming that it comes from an all-knowing, benevolent deity. If an omniscient and loving God tells us something, then we have good reason to believe it; since he is all-knowing, he would know the truth and would be unlikely to deceive us because he is benevolent. The problem is that one cannot prove noncircularly that any particular piece of writing is the word of God. And even those who agree that some particular scripture (for example, the New Testament) is the word of God frequently disagree on what the scripture means. I have found no straightforward condemnation of abortion or euthanasia in my copy of the Bible, and many devout Christians do not believe these practices to be condemned by God. In addition, there is no straightforward biblical claim that the soul is present at conception, and many Christians believe that ensoulment takes place much later. If those who accept these writings as scripture cannot even agree on what it commands or condemns, then an appeal to scripture as evidence will be even weaker when confronting those who do not accept the text as the expression of divine will. God's authority would be very strong evidence, but, alas, we have only the authority of ordinary humans that a certain text (and a certain interpretation of that text) represents God's authority.

IS HUMAN LIFE MERELY PHYSICAL, OR IS IT ALSO SPIRITUAL?

The science of biology must leave out any talk of the soul as a nonphysical thing, since biology is an empirical science and, as such, studies the physical world (specifically, living organisms and their physical processes) through observation. The Judeo-Christian notion of the soul is that of a nonphysical entity, which cannot be observed through the senses or any mechanical substitute for the senses (such as an electron microscope or a functional MRI). Thus, physical organisms must be explained—at least insofar as they *are* physical organisms—purely through physical causes. But those with a religious frame of mind might say that the human is more than a physiological organism. The naturalists will say yes, the human being is also a *social* being, and so can be studied (and explained) by the social sciences, such as cultural anthropology or psychology. These social sciences are still based on observation—specifically, observation of behavior.

Those with a religious worldview will say that the human being also includes something beyond the biological and the psychological; it also includes something "transcendent." The naturalists can say that there may be a soul, but whether or not there is a soul has no bearing on what we know— biology and psychology can leave it out; and if the soul does exist, then its existence is of no consequence for our biological and psychological understanding of what makes human beings alive. Those with the religious worldview might respond that there is evidence besides observable evidence. There is more to what we can know about human beings than just the biological and psychological facts. And so the argument goes around and around without making any real progress.

THE NEED FOR
COMMON GROUND

Because the two groups have such widely divergent articles of faith, there is no common ground from which to debate the most basic issues, such as what it is to be a human being or what life is. The result is a gap between the secular pro-choicers with their naturalistic view of life and the religious pro-lifers with their supernatural view of life. The naturalists want to argue on their terms, according to their articles of faith. But they would then be sure to win the argument, for religious claims are going to be ruled out because they cannot be justified by observation. On the other hand, the religious pro-lifers want to frame the issue according to articles of faith, which includes things that the naturalists reject. Victory for the religious pro-lifers would be all but guaranteed when they are arguing on their turf. But it is a hollow victory because the naturalist will dispute the outcome, claiming that the religious pro-lifer cheated by arguing from mere faith and not from things that can be observed.

What we have cannot even be characterized as a draw or a stalemate but more as a situation where one side is playing checkers and the other is playing chess. They might be playing on the same eight-by-eight-square checkered board—just as the religious pro-lifer and the secular pro-choicer are both talking about abortion—but they are making different moves, using different sorts of pieces, and playing by very different rules. There are not enough elements in common, and we end up in a situation where both sides claim victory even though no game is actually being played.

What we need is a common playing field where both sides can give their arguments and present their position in terms that the other can accept. They can only discuss and debate their views meaningfully in a forum where the rules do not exclude the pieces or the moves that each side needs to defend its claims. Also, the rules must not allow pieces or moves that one side will reject as invalid. What we need are elements that can be accepted by both sides. That will allow them to meet on fair ground and will not give an undeserved advantage to either side from the start.

PHILOSOPHY TO THE RESCUE

Philosophy, I argue, can provide that neutral playing field for the debate to take place between those with radically different perspectives. Philosophy can provide the forum in which both sides can get a fair shake and present their case. What is it about philosophy that makes this possible? It is the fact that philosophy itself has *no* articles of faith, no fundamental commitments of its own. Nothing is automatically included in its domain. Then again, nothing is automatically excluded either. Philosophy is pure critical thinking in which everything is fair game for questioning, even questions about what philosophy is and how it should be done.

For this reason, philosophy can take seriously the possibility of an immortal nonphysical soul, as well as the possibility of an all-powerful creator who put that soul into the physical body. Philosophy cannot dogmatically insist on the existence of such a soul, but neither can it dogmatically deny its existence. On the other hand, philosophy can take seriously the possibility that the human body is nothing more than an organic physical mechanism (albeit a very complicated one) as well as the possibility that this mechanism was not designed by some creator-deity but is merely the cumulative result of blind evolution. Either theory presents a distinct possibility until it is proven false or until a competing incompatible theory is proven true. Both views can be considered on their own merits—not from the perspective of the view itself, which would give it an undeserved advantage —but from a neutral perspective, with little if any axioms or basic commitments. We might not be able to consider the issue from *no* perspective, but we can consider it from a minimalist perspective, one that is based only on those basic beliefs that both sides agree upon.

PHILOSOPHY'S ARTICLES
OF FAITH: LOGIC

So far I have explained only in negative terms why philosophy can bridge the gap between these very different worldviews. I have described only what is absent from philosophy, how it lacks the reliance on faith that would serve as an obstacle to fairly considering positions that spring from fundamentally different belief systems. This is important because these obstacles need to be identified and eliminated in order to have a rational, critical discussion. But we also need to have a positive account of how to proceed once we remove these obstacles. It is like when my doctor told me I had high cholesterol. He gave me a long list of foods to eliminate from my diet. This list seemed to include just about every kind of food there is, and so it was not very helpful. I had to ask him, "What kind of food *can* I eat?" Similarly, we need to ask, "What do philosophers do that allows them to assess the relative merits of two very different perspectives?" Once we get them on the same playing field, where neither has an undeserved advantage, then what?

Philosophy involves analyzing concepts and constructing and assessing arguments. By "argument," of course, I do not simply mean debate or disagreement. I am using this term in the logical sense. An argument draws a conclusion that is justified on the basis of some body of evidence. In a logical argument there are *premises*: statements that are known or assumed to be true. There is also a *conclusion*, which, if the argument is good, follows from the truth of the premises. In some arguments the conclusion *must* be true if the premises are true. In a weaker type of argument the conclusion is merely more likely to be true (though not necessarily true) if the premises are true. In the first case (when there is a very strong connection between the truth of the premises and the truth of the conclusion) we have what is called a *deductive* argument. For example,

(1) All living humans have a soul.
(2) Mr. Smith is a living human being.
(3) Therefore, Mr. Smith has a soul.

This argument is a valid deductive argument. If the premises (1) and (2) are true, then the conclusion (3) must be true; it cannot possibly be false. The naturalists would agree that the argument is valid; they would agree that *if* the premises were true, *then* the conclusion would follow. However, the naturalist might reject one of the premises as being false, especially the claim that every living human has a soul. This example should drive home the importance of the need to find a neutral playing field. That means starting from premises that both sides can accept as true or probably true.

Deductive arguments like the one above tend to result in obvious conclusions. So it is unlikely that anything interesting regarding the issues concerning us will be determined by deductive arguments. Weaker but usually more informative arguments are *inductive*. For an inductive argument, if the premises are true, then the conclusion is probably true, though it is still possible (however unlikely) that it might be false.

For example:

    (1) I left a beer in the freezer last night

    (2) When beer freezes it expands.

    (3) If the beer expands, it will explode the bottle.

    (4) Therefore, there must be a big mess waiting for me in the freezer this morning.

The conclusion, that there is a mess in my freezer, is probably true, but it could be false. It is possible that the power went out last night, and so my freezer was not running.

Philosophers identify bad or very weak arguments by identifying *fallacies*. A fallacy is a mistake in reasoning. For example, consider the following argument:

    (1) If Mr. Smith committed the murder, then he will not have a good alibi for the night of the thirteenth.

    (2) Mr. Smith does not have a good alibi for the night of the thirteenth.

    (3) Therefore, Mr. Smith must have committed the murder.

The argument is invalid because the conclusion does not follow from the premises. The conclusion is not even more *likely* to be true if the premises are true. Maybe Mr. Smith has no alibi because he spent a quiet evening alone at home and went to bed early. The conclusion is not even probably true, for thousands of people in the city will have no alibi for the night of the thirteenth, but certainly they did not all commit the murder! This argument commits the fallacy that philosophers call *affirming the consequent* because premise (2) asserts the second part of the "if . . . then . . ." statement in premise (1). We could spend the length of this book covering all of the traditional fallacies and their fancy names, leaving no room to get to the issue at hand. Instead I shall point out and explain mistakes in reasoning as we happen upon them in the course of our inquiry.

DEFINITIONS AND THE MEANING OF TERMS

Carefully defining the terms used in the discussion and the concepts that these terms signify is necessary for any assessment of the validity or probability of an argument or system of beliefs. Much confusion and many bad arguments are based on lack of clarity about the terms being used. If terms are ill defined, then their meaning is vague (i.e., unclear or imprecise) or ambiguous (i.e., having more than one distinct meaning). A careful definition of the terms, and a complete description of the concepts they express, are essential in philosophy and can help to discover sloppiness or mistakes in what would otherwise seem to be valid reasoning. Consider the following:

(1) Doctors should render assistance at accident scenes where people are injured.
(2) Professor Meyers has witnessed a serious accident with injuries.
(3) Professor Meyers is a doctor.
(4) Therefore, Professor Meyers should render assistance to the people injured in the accident.

This is not the proper conclusion. Professor Meyers should call an ambulance! The word "doctor" in the first sentence was certainly intended to refer to *medical* doctors, not those with a PhD in philosophy. I doubt that philosophical analysis is going to be much help to someone with a broken leg.

Some terms that are going to need careful definition for our purposes are *life*, *person*, and *soul*. Anyone who claims that the word *life* has one unambiguous meaning has not thought very seriously about the matter. *Life* can mean "being biologically alive," and in this sense the fetus certainly has life. But if I write a biography titled *The Life of Abraham Lincoln*, I am certainly not talking about *life* in the biological sense. I would not fill the book with details about his heartbeat or his digestive processes or cell divisions. By *life* I mean the narrative constituted by the actions he performed and the events he experienced. The fetus has no life in this sense, and I would not start the biography of Lincoln with what he did while in his mother's womb. (I might say something about his parents in order to set the stage for his biography, but I would consider this background rather than part of his actual life—and I would not bother with exactly how or when he was conceived.)

No arguments are going to be won by definition alone. I could define abortion as "the murdering of an innocent fetal person in the womb," and thus conclude that abortion is wrong. But choosing to use the words in a certain way does not prove anything. This is clearly a loaded definition that defenders of abortion would reject. First of all, the word *murder* means "wrongful, intentional killing," but the word *abortion* does not mean wrongful killing (and if it did, then those who support the right of a woman to terminate her pregnancy would not use that word to describe the procedure but instead would find some other word with no moral connotation). Second, abortion defenders would question whether the fetus is a *person*. In order to make constructive arguments we need definitions that can be accepted by both sides and that do not make controversial claims true by definition. Rarely will a substantive dispute like the morality of abortion be settled by definition alone, no matter how good the definition is. But clear definitions, on which both sides can agree, are necessary for a meaningful discussion about the topic at hand. The pro-lifers can claim that abortion is wrong and that it is murder, but this is something they have to show through rational argumentation. They cannot just define it as being true.

Putting more into the definition than just the meaning of the word is a common mistake. In the abortion debate, the religious pro-lifer may try to define the term *alive* as meaning "having an immortal soul." Victory then might come easily for their position, but it would be a victory undeserved, for the naturalist would reject this definition of the word. Even if the naturalist believes in the soul, he will deny that that is what the word *alive* means. The naturalist could point out that if there is no soul, then, according to the loaded definition, *nothing* is alive. The existence of the soul is a matter of debate, but surely no one will disagree that you and I are alive!

One difficulty with definitions is that they are not so much discovered as invented. We can discover what definitions for a word have already been established by looking it up in the dictionary. (This is what we might call a *lexical* definition.) Even dictionary definitions can be determined by discovering how competent speakers in fact use the word (and that is how the meaning of words can change gradually through use). But at some point the meaning of a word was just made up by someone. It was an arbitrary decision to formulate some concept and then associate it with some sound or combination of letters.

Since words are ultimately invented, we can assign whatever meaning we want to a word. Assigning a new definition to a word is called a *stipula-*

tive definition, and it is perfectly acceptable in philosophy as long as it is understood to be a stipulative definition. For example, I can stipulate that by the word *alive* I mean "capable of growth, self-repair, and reproduction." That is what I mean when I use the term. But I cannot thereby dictate what others mean when they use the term *alive*. They might stipulate their own definition. Then we would have two different words that we would have to distinguish from each other. "Alive-B" would be my biologically defined term (having powers of growth, nutrition, cell division, etc.), and "alive-S" would be their spiritually defined term (possessing a supernatural soul). These two terms are not synonymous, although they might be coextensive (i.e., it might turn out that everything that is alive-S is also alive-B and vice versa, but that is something that would have be shown to be the case).

Stipulative definitions are more helpful than it might seem at first glance. Those who don't believe in the existence of a soul would want to say that nothing is alive-S, while some religious pro-lifers might want to say that humans are alive-S (and alive-B) and other animals and plants are merely alive-B. Thus, stipulative definitions are very useful for distinguishing and clearly labeling concepts that might otherwise be confused with one another. Without explaining and clearly defining our terms, confusion reigns. One might say that "it is always wrong to end the life of a living human being" and another might say that "it is not always wrong to end a human life." If one of them means it is always wrong to end a life-S and the other means it is sometimes OK to end a life-B, then their claims do not contradict each other; they are not even talking about the same thing.

FALSE STARTS: PRO-LIFE SIDE

Now that we have some idea of what an argument is, we can look at some especially weak arguments in the pro-life/pro-choice debate. By looking at what is wrong with obviously bad arguments we can get an idea of the features a good argument would have to have. This will also help us to make a fresh start when we begin our serious philosophical analysis of the moral issues with abortion. Just as a cook needs to wash the dishes and put away the utensils before he can cook in an uncluttered kitchen, we, too, should clean up our work space by sweeping out the garbage of misleading slogans and fallacies that are so prevalent in the debate that they cannot be ignored.

One rhetorical stratagem employed by activists is to appeal to our emotions. By getting us to feel certain emotions about an issue, activists try to get us to agree with their view. Appeals to emotions are not always inappropriate or misleading. Those who want to eliminate world hunger often show pictures of starving people in the hopes of moving us to open our wallets and donate to the cause. This is not misleading because we all know that starving from lack of food is a very bad thing and should be prevented. (I have never heard of anyone advocating a *pro-hunger* stance.) The appeal to emotions in this case merely motivates us to do what we already know we should do.

Pro-life advocates often resort to similar emotional appeals when they show pictures of aborted fetuses to make us squeamish about the idea of terminating pregnancy. Or, in a less gruesome strategy, they show pictures of live fetuses whose infantile features trigger our natural protective instincts. The problem with such tactics is that, although they may be effective, they do not provide any evidence or reasons for thinking that abortion is wrong. Just because we cannot stomach the image of a particular activity does not in any way mean it is wrong. If I were shown images of a tooth extraction, I would be horrified; but of course that does not mean that it is morally wrong to get a tooth removed.

Perhaps a better analogy is the practice of preparing and eating meat. Pictures from a slaughterhouse of chickens being killed, gutted, plucked, and disassembled might *motivate* one to become a vegetarian, but it does not provide a *reason* for thinking that eating meat is wrong. Of course, there may be reasons why we should not eat meat (for example, it causes unnecessary suffering to the animals, it is bad for the environment, etc.). But the pictures simply cause a visceral reaction, and this reaction is not necessarily appropriate or justified. And of course, people who were raised on a farm or grew up hunting might not have any negative reaction to the images. Similarly, there may be good reasons why abortion is wrong. But the pictures, and our emotional reaction to them, are not reasons.

Another tactic pro-life activists use for motivating an antiabortion response is to cite the numbers of abortions that are being performed. These numbers tend to be much higher that people expect, and those high numbers are intended to shock. The shock that is created is then supposed to motivate people to oppose legalized abortion. This tactic might succeed in rallying the pro-life troops, but it is irrelevant to whether abortion is wrong or should be legal. For if abortion is wrong, it is surely not because of how often it occurs.

If abortion is morally wrong, then *every single* abortion is wrong. If, on the other hand, abortion is not wrong, then it does not matter how often it occurs. The numbers *are* relevant to showing the severity of the social problems that abortion represents. For the pro-lifers, the high number signifies a serious social problem only because they are already convinced that abortion is morally wrong. But for the pro-choicer, the high number of abortions is a symptom of other social problems, such as poor education or a lack of easy access to contraception.

SLIPPERY SLOPE

Some of the tactics of the pro-life activists are more than mere slogans or shocking pictures. There are real arguments. Unfortunately, some of the arguments are poorly formulated. One particularly common argument is what philosophers and logicians call the *slippery slope* argument. One version of this argument claims that an action or policy will inevitably start an incremental chain of similar actions or policies that will eventually result in some highly undesirable actions or absurd policies. We might call this the *causal* version of the slippery slope. An example of this is seen in the claim that marijuana is a "gateway drug." The idea is that someone who is allowed to try marijuana will then try amphetamines and then cocaine and so on. The inevitable result will be a strung-out crackhead living on the streets and selling his organs for a fix. The conclusion is that we must not allow people to try marijuana, that by doing so, we're pretty much letting them get hooked on crack cocaine. The problem, of course, is that this chain of events is not even likely, let alone inevitable. Although it is true that most crack addicts start out smoking marijuana before turning to hard drugs, it is *not* true that most people who try marijuana eventually try crack, let alone end up as homeless junkies.

The other version of the slippery slope is not about chains of events but about what follows, logically, from a particular belief or policy. The idea is that if we accept a particular claim or principle, then we will be logically committed to accepting other similar claims or principles, which commit us to other progressively less plausible claims or principles. An amusing example of this can be found in the Old Testament when God tells Abraham that he intends to destroy Sodom. Abraham asks God if he would spare the city if there were fifty good men living there. God says he would. But if he would save it for fifty, Abraham asks, wouldn't he also save it for forty-five? After all, there is no morally significant difference between forty-five and fifty. It should be obvious where Abraham's line of reasoning goes. Once you start reasoning this way, the inevitable conclusion seems to be that you must spare the city even if only *one* good person lives there. The problem is that any cutoff point is arbitrary. Suppose God said that he would save the city for seventeen good men but not for sixteen. There is no reasonable way to justify that particular number. The only clear cutoff is between one and zero.

The slippery slope applies to the abortion issue in the following way. We would all agree that killing a newborn baby would be morally wrong (barring some very unusual circumstances, such as the baby being anencephalic). Then we must also conclude that it would be wrong to kill a nine-month-old fetus just prior to birth, since there is no significant difference between the fetus/baby just before birth and just after birth. (One big difference is that the baby begins to breathe only after birth, but that does not seem to be of great *moral* importance.) But if it is wrong to kill the fetus at nine months, then it is wrong to kill it at eight and a half months. And if it is wrong to kill it at eight and a half months, then it is wrong to kill it at eight months. The slippery slope argument continues along this line, arguing that since there is no significant difference between each stage of the fetus (or embryo) and the immediately previous stage—all the way down to the level of a single fertilized egg—there is thus no significant difference between the single fertilized egg and the newborn baby. The only point at which there is a significant difference is between the fertilized egg and the sperm-egg combination before fertilization. Before the egg is fertilized by the sperm, there is not yet a complete human, individual set of DNA.

Here is the problem with the slippery slope argument against abortion. Although it is true that fetal development is a continuum, with only gradual changes from stage to stage, that does not mean there are no morally significant changes from the fertilized egg to the fully developed fetus. These changes are not merely quantitative—the fetus does not simply grow larger with more cells—they are *qualitative* changes. The fetus develops new properties. Cells don't just multiply; they also specialize, forming new organs. Of course, there is no one point at which the fetus suddenly jumps from being a mere clump of cells to a fully formed, sentient human person. Nevertheless, that does not mean that there is no significant difference between an embryo of a few hundred cells and a nine-month-old fetus. There are significant cutoff points, even if they are inexact or approximate cutoffs.

The pro-choicer can say that performing an abortion would be wrong (unless necessary to save the life of the mother) in the third trimester but not wrong in the first trimester. The second trimester, when the fetus is starting to be viable outside the womb and the brain is starting to function, might be an indeterminate gray area. Perhaps an exact cutoff point—before which abortion would be OK but after which it would be wrong—is unavoidably arbitrary. But it is only arbitrary in its exactness. We can provide reasons for distinguishing early term abortions from late-term abortions, even if we cannot determine an exact moment dividing them.

We make and enforce all sorts of arbitrary cutoffs in the law. Take, for example, speed limit laws. We could apply the slippery slope argument and say that if it is safe to drive at 55 mph, then surely it is safe to drive at 56 mph. And if 56 mph is safe, then so is 57 mph. Surely 1 mph faster is not going to make a big difference. But if we follow this line of reason all the way to its absurd conclusion, then we would have to say that driving at 90 mph is perfectly safe. We should have no speed limit laws! But although there is no great difference between 55 mph and 56 mph, there is a *huge* difference between 55 mph and 90 mph. And while 55 mph (as opposed to 54 or 56) might be somewhat arbitrary, it is not entirely without reason.

Another problem with the slippery slope is that it cuts both ways. We could start by saying that if 90 mph is unsafe, then so is 89 mph. The inevitable conclusion would be that the speed limit should be zero! That would certainly reduce traffic fatalities. Similarly, the pro-choicer could start by claiming that the fertilized egg is just one cell. Surely there is nothing wrong with killing one human cell. And if it is OK to destroy the embryo at one cell, then it is OK to destroy it at two cells—all the way up to nine months. This pro-choice slippery slope is just as invalid as the pro-life version.

FALSE STARTS: PRO-CHOICE SIDE

There are, of course, slogans and bad arguments on the pro-choice side as well. One slogan sometimes heard by pro-choicers is that abortion is a "private decision" and so only concerns the pregnant woman and her physician. It is no one else's business. The problem with this claim is that it already assumes that the fetus is not a person or a potential person—a claim the pro-lifer would certainly reject. The pro-lifer could claim that it *is* someone else's business: It is the business of the fetus that is going to be aborted! If we could assume that the fetus has no interest at stake and does not count in our moral deliberation, then it might follow that abortion is not morally wrong. But that is not something that can simply be assumed. It must be shown through some sort of argument.

Another common pro-choice slogan is "It's my body, so I can do what I want with it." Like most slogans, this is an oversimplification of the issue. If what is meant is that the *fetus* is part of the woman's body, like a spleen or an appendix or a tumor, then the claim seems to be false (unless we can show that the fetus is not its own person or potential person). Perhaps what is meant is that the uterus is part of the woman's body, and so she can do what she wants with it, including emptying it of its contents. Though there may be something to this (which we will consider in chapter 8), the slogan is at best a caricature of an argument. For it seems obvious that you do not have a right to do *anything* you want with your own body, especially if doing so will likely result in harm to another person. I do not have a right to recklessly swing my elbows around on a crowded subway, knowing that doing so is likely to injure my fellow passengers. If the fetus counts for nothing morally, then it would follow that it is only the woman's own body. But, again, this cannot be assumed without argument.

ANALYSIS OF WORLDVIEWS

How does logic apply to an analysis of worldviews? A system of beliefs can be defective in many ways. To start, it can be logically inconsistent. An inconsistent set of beliefs is one in which some of the beliefs entail the falsity of one or more of the other beliefs in the set. So not all of the beliefs can be true, which is to say that some of the beliefs must be false. A system of beliefs that necessarily contains false beliefs is a defective system, and so must be altered to be consistent. If that is not possible, then it must be rejected entirely.

A system of beliefs can also be defective if it is incoherent. It is hard to give an exact definition of incoherence, but an incoherent set of beliefs, we might say, is one that "does not hold together." Sets of beliefs are sometimes incoherent because they undermine each other or because there are obvious gaps that cannot easily be filled. Conspiracy theories are often suffer from these sorts of flaws. For example, there are some who claim that the Freemasons are involved in a secret plot to control the US government and create some sort of "new world order." As evidence, they point to Masonic symbols on US currency and on the Great Seal of the United States. The problem with this theory is that if there is a secret plot, it does not make any sense for them to offer up these symbols as clues that might give away their scheme.

These are just some of the ways that philosophers can clarify and assess theories and analyze and critique arguments. These methods—defining terms, assessing the consistency and coherency of sets of beliefs, and critiquing arguments—apply to any and all theories. By "theory" we do not necessarily mean an all-encompassing worldview or a complete science of everything. It can simply be an explanation of one thing. For example, one might have a theory of why Brutus helped to kill Caesar, or a theory of what Joyce's *Ulysses* is really about, or a theory of how the universe began. Any such theory faces two possible sources of inconsistency or incoherence. It may be internally inconsistent (or incoherent) or it may be externally inconsistent (or incoherent). By *internally* inconsistent I mean that the beliefs that make up the theory conflict with each other. By *externally* inconsistent I mean that the theory is not consistent with other things that we know or have very good reason to believe. If a theory is internally inconsistent, then it must be rejected as false or modified to eliminate the inconsistencies. If a theory is externally inconsistent, then we will have to decide which is more important, the theory or those other beliefs that contradict it.

CONCLUSION

Now that we have some notion of what philosophy is, we can begin to analyze, in an unbiased way, the respective theories of life held by many on each side of the abortion issue and then assess them on their own grounds as well as determine how they fit with other things about which most people on both sides agree.

SUGGESTED FURTHER READING

Maguire, Daniel C. *Sacred Choices: The Right to Contraception and Abortion in Ten World Religions*. Minneapolis: Fortress Press, 2001.

CHAPTER 2

WHAT IS THE SOUL?

Many nonphilosophers believe that abortion is morally wrong because they accept what we have called the *sanctity of life* principle. The sanctity of life principle states that the intentional killing of any human being is morally wrong. This principle comes from the Catholic Church, although it is also held by some, but not all, Christians of other denominations. According to this view it is wrong to intentionally end the life of any human being, even one who is not yet fully developed or no longer capable of thought or experience, or even if the human being in question deserves it. Some who hold the sanctity of life principle are inconsistent on this last point, but the Catholic Church officially disapproves of capital punishment because it violates the sanctity of life. The principle holds that all living human life is sacred because each living human being has a soul from the moment of conception until the moment all life ceases.

SUBSTANTIVE VERSUS SEMANTIC OR CONCEPTUAL QUESTIONS

In order to test this principle, we need to ask the obvious question "What is the soul?" But, in a technical sense, this is *not* really the question we need to ask. As the question is stated, it seems to assume that the soul exists and that we are inquiring into its nature and its essential properties. The question we need to ask, then, is not substantive; it is not an inquiry into the thing that we call a "soul." We would have to already be able to point to something and agree that this is a soul, and then examine it. Examples of questions of this substantive sort might be "What exactly is lightning?" or "What is this strange meat-like product they serve in the cafeteria?" or even "What does this word *zymurgy* mean?" But our inquiry into soul cannot proceed this way, for all sides do not agree on the existence of the soul, and we have no sample before us that we can examine.

Unless we can agree that souls exist, and agree that a particular entity that we can examine is a soul, the question is not so much what a soul *is* but rather what a soul *would be* if it existed. The question may turn out to be like the question "What is a black hole?" Theories about black holes existed long before there was any observation of black holes. In fact, it is only once the notion of a black hole was clearly defined and described that we could know what to look for in trying to find one.

On the other hand, the question of what a soul is may turn out to be more like the question "What is a witch?" In some sense, the answer is *nothing*; a witch is not anything because witches do not exist. Since there are no witches, they can have no nature, no essential properties. In another sense, however, we *can* answer the question "What is a witch?" even under the assumption that they do not exist. If I say, "There are no witches," it is not meaningless for one of my listeners to ask me, "What is a witch?" and for me to answer him. He is asking what it is that I am claiming does not exist. For me to say that something does not exist, I must be able to say what that thing is that does not exist. In other words, I must be able to describe these nonexisting things. In describing a witch, I give its properties—not the properties that witches actually have but the properties they would have if they existed.

Thus, when we ask what a witch is, what we are really asking is what do we mean by the term *witch*? When I describe the properties that witches would have if they existed, I am giving a meaning of the term *witch*—a definition, which is a list of the criteria for being a witch. (This definition leaves it open whether there is anything that actually satisfies these criteria.) I can describe a witch as an evil woman who practices black magic, flies around on a broomstick, turns sleeping men into horses and rides them to exhaustion, and may or may not have warts and green skin. This description is important even if it only gives the meaning of the word and there are no actual things that fit this description. Besides the use of this word in fairy stories and other fictions, my friend might think that I'm using the term *witch* metaphorically to describe a mean woman, as in "My boss is a real witch!" He might insist that witches of this later sort exist but agree that witches of the other sort—the fairy tale witches that live in gingerbread houses and eat children—do not exist.

So there are two distinct meanings to questions of the form "What is X?" The first is a description or analysis of the concept X, essentially a definition of the term *X*. The second form of the question "What is X?" inquires into the nature of some actually existing thing X. What properties does this thing have? The first question can be merely stipulated. But it could also be a philosophical endeavor if we want to find a *good* definition and evaluate the adequacy or coherence of the definition. At any rate, we need to give some answer to the first question ("What does 'X' mean?") before we can even decide whether any Xs exist, let alone what particular things are Xs. We need to know how to recognize an X when we stumble upon one.

The second question is the substantive question. For it to be answered (and, indeed, for us to even be able to ask it), the first question must be answered, if only in a vague and preliminary way. The substantive questions can still be philosophical, such as when we make a rational inquiry into the nature of the Good. First we need to define *good*, perhaps as "that which we ought to pursue or prefer." That is a philosophical question about the meaning of the term *good*, a philosophical analysis of the concept designated by the word. Good things are things that are worthy of pursuit. Now the question is *which* things are worthy of pursuit? This is also a philosophical question, though it is a substantive philosophical question, not a mere conceptual philosophical question.

THE CONCEPT OF THE SOUL

In order to assess the sanctity of life principle, we need to ask what the soul is. In other words, what do we mean by "soul"? This analysis of the concept of the soul is important for several reasons. First, our conception of the soul may be self-contradictory, in which case there can be no such soul. Or it may be hopelessly vague, in which case we wouldn't know a soul if it bit us in the ass. Second, there may be multiple conceptions of the soul, and so the soul may exist according to one definition but not exist according to another.

Finally, we need a clear idea of the concept of the soul to see what we can infer from it; especially what moral claims would follow from the existence of such a soul.

A lot of confusion is caused by not clearly defining our terms or analyzing our concepts. It is necessary to be clear what we are talking about in order to avoid confusion and equivocation. Equivocation is when we unwittingly or intentionally use two different senses of the same word as if we were talking about one concept. (See chapter 1.) For example, consider this argument.

(1) Anyone who steals is a criminal and should be punished.
(2) Today at recess, Johnny stole second base.
(3) Therefore, Johnny is a criminal and should be punished.

In the first statement, "stealing" means taking (by force or by stealth) property that rightfully belongs to another person without her consent. In the second sentence, "stealing" refers to a maneuver in baseball, which is allowed by the rules of the game and is morally insignificant. The argument works only if "stealing" is used in the same way in both statements. (The argument would be valid it Johnny removed the base from the infield and took it home when no one was watching.)

Precisely defining our terms can show that apparent disagreements are not disagreements at all (or that apparent agreements are not real agreements). Two different people might both insist that the human soul really exists. They seem to agree and seem to be saying the same thing. But one of them might have one conception of the soul (we will call it soul-1), while the other has a markedly different conception (soul-2). Thus one of them says that soul-1 exists, and the other says soul-2 exists. There is no agreement but only apparent agreement because they are not making the same claim. It is possible that soul-1 is real but soul-2 is not (or vice versa). As we shall soon see, this is actually the case in the history of philosophy. Different philosophers have argued for the existence of distinctly different entities that are all traditionally referred to as "soul."

For some, "soul" means something physical; for others it means something purely spiritual (though it is not exactly clear what that means, since *spirit* is just another word for *soul*). Some believe it is something eternal; others have held that the soul can be destroyed or that it ceases to exist when the body dies. For some it is the seat of consciousness, while for others it is just a blind force. Of course, there is some core notion, however vague, that all of these different concepts have in common and that makes us inclined to refer to them each as "soul." But we are concerned more with the differences than with their similarities, for we are looking for the particular conception of soul implied by, or appealed to with, the sanctity of life principle.

We could probably fill an entire book much longer than this one with nothing more than descriptions of the different notions of soul—both from various religious and theological traditions (Judeo-Christian, Hindu, voodoo, Shinto, as well as the various indigenous religions) and from the various philosophical theories (Democritus, Plato, Plotinus, the Stoics, Saint Thomas Aquinas, Leibniz, Kant, Hegel, Kierkegaard, etc.).

Instead of an unnecessary catalog of every concept of soul, I will focus on two prominent philosophers and their respective theories about the soul—Aristotle and Descartes. I choose these two thinkers for three reasons. First, they have radically different descriptions of what the soul is. Second, they are enormously important thinkers who have both significantly shaped modern Western thought (including Christian thought, even though they are not theologians). Finally, the prominent Judeo-Christian notion of the soul (or at least the notion that seems to be implied by sanctity of life) combines certain elements of both theories while rejecting other features from each.

To be precise, of course, neither Aristotle nor Descartes ever used the word *soul*. Descartes wrote in both Latin and his native French and so used the terms *anima* and *l'ame*, while Aristotle wrote in ancient Greek hundreds of years before anything like the English language was spoken and so he used the Greek term *psyche*. Nevertheless, all of these terms translate roughly into our English word *soul*—or at least they have been and continue to be translated that way. And though Aristotle and Descartes disagree strongly in their conception of the soul, each of these concepts has enough in common with our concept that it is reasonable that we should use the same the word. If we want to be precise, however, we should distinguish between the Aristotelian-soul, the Cartesian-soul, and the concept of soul that seems to be held by those who appeal to it as religious grounds for opposing abortion.

ARISTOTLE'S CONCEPT
OF THE SOUL

For Aristotle, understanding an entity requires one to grasp its "form," or essence. Aristotle believed that these forms were real, but that they did not exist on their own. They were properties of things or *substances*. A substance, in the philosophical sense of the term, is something that exists on its own, as opposed to a property, which must be the property *of* something. A rock is a substance; the hardness of the rock is a property and not a substance because the hardness cannot exist without the rock.

For Aristotle, substances have a dual nature. They are composed of *matter* (the stuff it is made of) and *form* (its essential properties or structure). A brick, for example, is made of a kind of matter (clay, or whatever it is that bricks are made out of), and form (the rectangular shape and hardness of the brick). If it were irregularly shaped, or if it were soft and crumbly, then it would be useless for constructing buildings, and so it would not really be a brick at all. Now a complete substance, like our brick, can also serve as the matter for some other more complex substance. The brick is a substance on its own, but it can also make up part of the matter of a house. The form of the house would be the design, the way the bricks and other materials are assembled to make a house. If a hurricane crushes this house (as recently happened to my neighbor's house), then the form is gone, and what we are left with is no longer a house but mere rubble.

Now, for Aristotle, the human being is, like all other substances, a composite of matter and form—the matter being the body, and the form being the soul. Of course, the body itself is already a substance and so is made of matter—the flesh, muscle, bone, and so on—and has its form: the structural anatomy that makes it a human body and not a mere mass of tissues. In other words, the form of the body is the general design. The skin is on the outside, the guts on the inside. The hip bone is connected to the leg bone; the leg bone is connected to the knee bone, and so on.

The soul, then, is the property of being alive or is a cluster of properties that constitute being alive. When the body takes on this property of being alive (the soul) then we have a living human being. The human person is body plus soul. The body is the matter, and the soul is the form, or essence of being alive. This soul then gives the living person powers that the mere body would not have on its own, such as the power to walk about, to talk, and to think. In the same way, once the design (the form) is imposed on the housing materials, that form gives it powers it did not have before, such as the power to provide shelter and protect the occupant's stuff. Anything that has a soul is alive, and without the soul it is dead. Of course, not just anything can have a soul. Only bodies made out of the right kind of stuff and arranged in the right kind of way can have a soul, just as you cannot make a house out of gelatin or hair or (as the three pigs learned) straw. This is a kind of *vitalism*, a belief in a special life-giving force. But it is a more sophisticated form of vitalism than the crude notion of some kind of vague physical life force held by ancient Greek common folk.

Since the soul is the property of being alive, Aristotle reasoned that all living things have a soul—not just humans but also other animals and even plants. But of course, since a human being is very different from a plant (and being alive for a human being means much more than it does for a plant), there must be different sorts of souls with different powers. The simplest souls are plant souls. These rudimentary souls include only the powers to perform the basic biological processes of growth, nutrition (i.e., taking elements from the environment and using them for energy), reproduction, and so on. All souls have these powers, which provide a base minimum for being a living biological organism. But plants have *only* these powers. Animals, on the other hand, also have the powers of sensation and directed self-movement. They can see and smell, and they can also run (or swim or fly) and hunt and mate. Humans alone have the additional power of intellect, which allows for rational thinking and moral deliberation.

It is important to keep in mind that, for Aristotle, soul is a form or essential attribute; it is the property or set of properties that make the physical human body into a living person. Thus the soul is not a substance, which means that it cannot exist without the body and so it must cease to exist when the person dies.

The question "Where does the soul go when we die?" does not make sense according to this view. It doesn't *go* anywhere. By analogy, the gable on the side of my house used to be a triangle. Hurricane Katrina sent a tree on top of my roof, partly crushing it. Now it is no longer a triangle. The question of "Where does the soul go?" would be analogous to "Where did the triangularity go when the roof was crushed?" The triangle that formed the side of my roof was not a substance; it was not one of the building materials along with the brick and wood. When those materials were violently rearranged, the property of being a triangle ceased to exist. Likewise, if the materials that make up the living human body are violently rearranged, then it is no longer alive and its soul no longer exists.

Let us summarize and analyze Aristotle's account of the soul. First of all, the soul is not a substance. It is not a thing that can exist on its own but is only a property or cluster of properties of the living thing. Thus it cannot exist after the person dies or before the person is born. Second, for Aristotle, the soul is not supernatural or nonphysical but consists of ordinary, natural properties or attributes. The basic powers of the soul that make any thing alive are the powers of growth, nutrition, reproduction—all purely biological processes that can be observed and explained according to natural laws. The same could also be said for the higher powers of sensation and reason that the human soul has. These, too, can be observed by observing a person's behavior.

ARISTOTLE AND THE SANCTITY OF LIFE

The soul, as Aristotle conceives it, is such that its presence in the body is sufficient (and necessary) for it to be alive. That means that if a body has a soul, then it is alive, and if it is alive, then it has a soul. It is the possession of soul, and nothing else, that constitutes being alive. In this way, Aristotle's view is a kind of vitalism. Some of the powers of the soul include growth and nutrition, and so any natural organism with these powers is alive. This means that, according to Aristotle's theory, humans would have a soul from the moment of conception, for it is from that moment that the fertilized egg can grow into a human being. Also, a person continues to have a soul until biologically dead—and that means when all biological functions, such as circulation of the blood (heartbeat) and breathing, cease. Being brain-dead for Aristotle would mean that one of the soul's powers—or several powers, such as sensation, self-movement, and reasoning—has been lost. There would be still be a soul, however, but it would more closely resemble the soul of a plant than the soul of a human being.

On the other hand, since the soul consists of physical properties identified with being biologically alive, Aristotle held that animals and even plants had souls, since they, too, are biologically alive. Presumably, if Aristotle had

had access to microscopes and had been aware of the existence of micro-organisms, he would have granted that even single-celled yeasts, algae, and protozoa have souls. Even tiny prokaryotic bacteria would have souls, though presumably viruses would not because they are not capable of engaging in any biological functions such as nutrition and reproduction on their own.

From this quick sketch we can see that Aristotle's theory of the soul will not at all support something like the sanctity of life principle. Although Aristotle would probably agree that the soul is present at conception and remains until all biological processes have ceased, he also thinks that animals and plants also have souls. The sanctity of life, if it means the sanctity of any living thing with a soul, would thus not allow for (intentionally) killing *any* living creature, even plants. It would be very difficult, though I suppose not impossible, for a human being to survive without killing any living thing. Obviously we would have to refrain from eating meat, but many people already do that, often for reasons involving the respect for life. But what about plants? Well, we could eat parts of plants without killing the plant itself by eating fruits, nuts, legumes, and other plant parts that could be harvested without killing the plant itself. We could also eat eggs and dairy products. For that matter we could even eat animal parts if they could be removed without killing the animal, as we do with crab claws. (Crab fishers remove one claw of the stone crab and then toss the crab back into the ocean where the claw will eventually grow back.) I suppose we could also eat things that die of their own accord, although I personally would rather go hungry.

One could consistently accept the Aristotelian notion of the soul and the sanctity of life principle if one were willing to adhere to such an unusual diet and to insist that others do so as well. But, more important, the Aristotelian theory does not give us any reason to think that possessing a soul grants a creature such a lofty moral status as an absolute right to life. For one, Aristotle's notion of the soul is not that of a supernatural or divine entity but merely a cluster of biological properties and potentials. Furthermore, those who accept the sanctity of life principle typically do not think that killing a carrot is as bad as aborting an early term fetus. Generally the sanctity of life refers to the sanctity of *human* life.

Of course, Aristotle thinks that the human soul is different from the soul of plants or even animals. The human soul has the power of intellect, and in that regard it is unique (as far as we know) among living creatures. For this reason Aristotle would agree that human beings have a special moral status, that killing a person is much worse than killing an animal or a plant. This, however, will not support the sanctity of (human) life principle, for this difference between humans and other creatures is not due to the presence or absence of a soul but due to the presence or absence of some power of the soul: the power of intellect. Although only humans have this power, not all humans do. A fetus does not have the power of reason, nor does someone in an irrevocable coma. It is not clear exactly what makes a being worthy of moral consideration in Aristotle's theory because Aristotle did not think in terms of moral rights or even moral duties. But it seems most reasonable, on a view like this, that what grants something special moral status is some kind of capacity or set of capacities, such as the capacity to think or feel. This is roughly the view held by many naturalists. It does not matter that for Aristotle these powers reside in the soul. The important point is that it is not the soul per se that makes a human being worthy of moral consideration but the powers *of* the soul.

RENÉ DESCARTES

Let us now consider a view of the soul that is very different from that of Aristotle, the theory put forth by René "I think, therefore I am" Descartes. I hope the reader will forgive me for skipping ahead two thousand years, but this is not a treatise on the history of philosophical theories about the soul. Our purpose here is simply to show that there are widely varying theories. Examining these different theories of the soul will also help us to formulate and describe the distinctively religious pro-life notion held by those who accept the sanctity of life. Given these intentions, we need only examine as many theories of the soul as are necessary to show this variety and to uncover enough details to flesh out the conception we want to examine. Aristotle, I believe, got us halfway there. Now Descartes' theory will bring us home.

Descartes was an interesting man, a true Renaissance man in the sense that he engaged in a wide variety of intellectual pursuits. Besides being one of the greatest (if not the greatest) philosophers of his time, Descartes was also a brilliant mathematician, an astronomer, and an amateur biologist. He even wrote a book on the art of fencing! He died prematurely in his mid-fifties because the queen of Sweden made him get up too early in the morning. (Not being a morning person myself, I have always felt a certain affinity with Descartes in this regard and have used the story of his demise as an excuse to never teach morning classes.)

Of special relevance for our purposes is Descartes' faith, or alleged faith. In his most important writings Descartes claims that what he has argued for is consistent with the teachings of the Church (which at that time meant the Roman Catholic Church) on matters of God and the soul. Some scholars have doubted Descartes' sincerity on this matter, chalking it up to his extreme fear of persecution and his tendency to be a self-promoter, seeking patronage wherever he could. Without strong evidence to the contrary, however, I see no reason why we should not take Descartes at his word and assume that he did not intend to contradict official Church dogma on any of the key issues. Of course, this is not to say that the Church agreed with Descartes' claim to be consistent with Catholic theology. In fact, his books were, for a long time, banned by the pope.

DESCARTES' PROJECT

Descartes' primary concern, as he tells us in his *Meditations on First Philosophy*, is to try to find something that is absolutely 100 percent certain, some piece of knowledge that can be known infallibly, without any possibility of error. The worry Descartes had is a deeply disturbing philosophical realization that we can know something without being 100 percent certain *that* we know it. Let me explain the difference between knowledge and certainty. Suppose someone asks me what is the largest country (in terms of landmass) in Africa. I say it is Sudan. Do I *know* that it is Sudan? Well, I believe that it is Sudan, and I have good reason to believe it: I read it in a well-respected book and have checked it on the map. I am not just guessing, in which case I would not have knowledge even if I were correct (it would be a lucky guess). So I believe it and I have evidence. That is usually considered to be sufficient for knowledge, as long as the belief is also true. But here is where we get to the sticky part. It might not be true despite all the evidence. Maybe the book I read is out of date; perhaps the borders have changed since the book was printed. (The borders may even have changed only minutes ago due to some treaty just recently signed). That is very unlikely, but it is *possible*. All we have is the evidence for our beliefs. We have no immediate access to the truth of those beliefs. So despite all of the evidence for our beliefs, they might be false.

For those reasons, Descartes wanted to find something he could know with absolute certainty, something he could not possibly be mistaken about. To do this, he goes through all of his beliefs and tries to find any possibility, no matter how strange and unlikely, that they might be false.

He starts with things that we know from observation. I may be mistaken about Sudan being the largest country in Africa, but what about things that I can see with my own eyes? Can't I be certain that this tree I am looking at is taller than that tree over there? I cannot at all be certain about that because the eyes can be deceived by optical illusions. What about our experiences as a whole? For example, right now you are reading this book. How do you know you are reading it? Because you are aware of yourself reading this book, in whatever place you happen to be. But, as Descartes points out, maybe you are not reading this book, maybe you are asleep right now and only dreaming that you are reading this book. Maybe there is no such book; it is just something you cooked up in your head. Of course, I am not likely to convince you that you are actually dreaming, for your experiences right now are certainly much more vivid and coherent than any dream. But some dreams are more vivid than others; maybe this is the most vivid and cohesive and detailed dream you have ever had. It is a very slim possibility, but it is not impossible. Of course, even if you are dreaming, your dreams are based on experiences from waking life, and it is those things that you might now claim that you can be certain of, even in your dreams. This might include beliefs about who you are, where you live, what your name is, or who your family is.

At this point Descartes resorts to the most fantastic and paranoid device ever conceived of in the history of philosophy: the "evil demon" argument. He asks us to consider the possibility that some evil demon with godlike powers has created an elaborate set of illusions in your mind. Your whole life has been one very long, coherent, vivid dream planted in your head by this malevolent supernatural being. None of it is real—your friends, your family, your home, your school and/or workplace, the earth itself—all figments of your imagination created by the evil demon.

Sounds impossible? No, just very, *very* unlikely. But it is possible. Consider the popular movie *The Matrix*. The main character, Neo, comes to find out that his whole life is fake. The world he experienced all of his life is nothing but an elaborate hoax generated by intelligent supercomputers. It is possible, but very unlikely, that something like that could actually be taking place. If we could not imagine that such a thing were possible, then the movie would not have been very interesting. Maybe you are in the Matrix right now. For that matter, if Neo had been somewhat more philosophically disposed, he would have realized that after leaving the Matrix, he might still be in the Matrix—it might be a *fake* outside, or a meta-Matrix. The whole experience of being liberated from it may have just been part of the story line that the computers created to keep him busy so that he would not *actually* escape.

This is basically Descartes' reasoning. Maybe you are in the Matrix right now; and if you are, then virtually all of your beliefs are false, even simple facts about who you are, where you live, what you have done in your life, and what you are doing right now. However, Descartes' evil demon argument takes this reasoning one step further—a very important step further. Neo had a real physical body, a body that was very like the body he experienced himself having while in the Matrix (except with shorter hair). It was his body that was plugged into the Matrix. It was his brain in that body that had those experiences of being other places and doing other things while in fact his body was lying passively in a pod filled with goo. What makes Descartes' evil demon scenario so different from science fiction examples of brains in vats or bodies hooked up to the Matrix is that the evil demon uses supernatural powers rather than high-tech gadgetry. Thus it is conceivable that the evil demon's victim (i.e., you) is not a body or physical brain hooked up to electrodes; instead you might have no body at all. Maybe you are just a spirit in some kind of purgatory without a body and are merely made to feel "physical" pleasure and pain and to experience the world *as if* you had a body. Instead of a body in a pod at the mercy of super-computers, you may be only a soul at the mercy of some supernatural prankster.

Descartes then asks, What can we know in this epistemological worst-case scenario? Well, you can still be certain at least that you exist. The demon could not make you falsely think that you exist when you do not exist, for if you did not exist, how could you be fooled into thinking that you did? There would be no *you* to be fooled. So here Descartes finds his one infallible, 100 percent certain belief. He can be certain of his own existence. You can be certain of your existence, but what is this *you* that exists? Normally you would describe yourself by describing your body (male/female, short/tall, etc.), your occupation, your hobbies, your friends, and your family. But all of these things could be an illusion planted by the evil demon. What is it about your existence that cannot be doubted, that you could know to be true even if there were an evil demon? Descartes says that you know you are a *thinking thing*. You might also have a body, and probably in fact do, but the mind is all you can be sure of.

DESCARTES' THEORY OF SOUL

Descartes refers to this "thinking thing" as a soul or a mind. (He uses the two interchangeably.) So for Descartes the soul is identified primarily, if not exclusively, with the intellect and the capacity for thinking. Unlike Aristotle's theory, biological powers of nutrition and growth are not essential to the soul on Descartes' theory, for we could imagine the soul existing without these powers. For Aristotle, thinking was merely one power of the soul among others. Descartes equates this soul (the mind) with the self. Who I am is essentially my soul, the thinking part of me, not so much the body, which I just happen to inhabit. For Aristotle, on the contrary, the human person is a unity of soul and body, each being necessary (though each in a different way) for the existence of the person.

More important, for Descartes, the soul is nonphysical and is a substance, not just a property. It thus differs in two key ways from Aristotle's idea that the soul *is* physical and *not* a substance but just a property (or set of properties). As a substance, the soul can exist independently of the body. Descartes' argument for this is rather clever. He points out first that we can imagine the soul existing independently of any physical body. After all, weren't we just now imagining the possibility of not having a body but merely being deceived into thinking so by an evil demon? If we can imagine it without too much difficulty, then it must be at least logically possible, (whether or not it is physically possible). And if it is logically possible, then it must be possible, for if there were an omnipotent God, then he could do anything logically possible. Since it is logically possible that the soul exist without the physical body, God could separate them. If they could be separated, then they must be distinct, independently existing entities.

This may seem like a desperate move, literally a deus ex machina, but this is not so. The argument does not depend on the existence of God, only on the idea of God. Even the atheist could admit that *if* an omnipotent God existed, *then* he could separate the soul from the body. Atheists and agnostics often do appeal to the idea of God in ways like this. For example, a quantum physicist, in order to make his point, might say that "even God could not determine both the velocity and the mass of the particle at the same time." And what the physicist means by this is that there is no objective truth to be known.

It might be helpful to contrast this with another example. Some things we cannot imagine separately, such as mere properties of things. Think of some particular courageous man. Now try to think of his courage being separated from him. I do not mean, think of him as having lost his courage (for the man can exist without the courage), but think of his courage continuing to exist separated from the person. That is something we cannot imagine because courage is not the kind of thing that can be thought of as a substance. (Even God could not separate the man and his courage this way, not because he lacks the power, but because it does not make any sense.) If my friend said to me, "There is some courage in the closet," I'd be baffled. Does he mean courageous *people*? Or maybe he is using "courage" in a different sense. (Maybe he is telling me he has a six-pack of John Courage Ale in there, and I can help myself!)

BODY AND SOUL

Since the soul, on Descartes' view, is not physical, it is not essentially concerned with the physical body nor the physiological processes of life, such as growth, nutrition, reproduction, and so on. It would not make sense for a *non*physical entity to be the source of all these *physical* phenomena. In fact, Descartes had a rather mechanistic view of the living organism and its physiological processes. In one of his writings, Descartes presents a theory of how the heart works, a theory based partly on dissecting animal hearts. His theory, unfortunately, is way off. (He credits heat as the cause of the beating rather than nerve impulses.) What is important about Descartes' account, and what it has in common with modern biological science, is that it is entirely mechanistic. The heart, and the body in general, is seen as a very complicated machine. We may not have gears or pulleys or electrical wiring in our bodies, but we have the biological and chemical equivalents of these. And our bodies work according to the same laws of nature as do human-made machines. Aristotle, on the contrary, held that even natural things have a goal (or *telos*) for which they naturally strive and which partly explains their motions. Aristotle appeals at some basic level to the mysterious potentiality or *powers* in his scientific explanations of the natural world. But Descartes, like modern scientists, tries to reduce these powers to more basic cause-and-effect explanations.

Since the soul, on Descartes' view, is identical with the intellect and thinking, anything that is conscious and rational must have a soul. Animals do not have a soul since they are not rational. Descartes also seemed to think that animals are not even conscious. Animals, he thought, were merely very sophisticated machines. They do not actually feel pain but are merely programmed, by some hardwired mechanism, to react to injury, much like the way a baby doll "cries" under certain conditions. (Let us hope that Monsieur Descartes did not have any pets!)

For Descartes the soul is identified with consciousness and the intellect. Many people, myself included, believe that it is consciousness that is (at least part of) what gives us obligations to other people; and the capacity for rational thought is one of the reasons that our obligations to humans is greater than our obligations to other animals. It is one of the reasons that I would save a person (even a hermit with no friends to mourn for him) over an animal (even if that animal were a cherished family pet). So, unlike Aristotle's view of the soul, having a soul of the Cartesian variety does seem to grant special moral status. We have obligations to thinking things that we do not have to merely feeling things.

Nevertheless, this view does not support the sanctity of life view any more than Aristotle's. The problem is that, although it is true that only humans have souls, it is not at all clear that every human has a soul. Soul is what makes a human being conscious; it is what does the thinking. But it is not what makes humans biologically alive. That can be explained by purely mechanical biological processes. Thus, on this view, it is perfectly possible to be biologically alive without having a soul. Animals are certainly no less alive than you or I— at least in the biological sense. Thus it is possible for someone to be brain-dead but still alive (as in the case of Terri Schiavo or Karen Ann Quinlan) and yet no longer have a soul. The soul might be gone while the heart still beats. And this might even explain why the person is in the persistent vegetative state. Destruction of the brain might be sufficient to separate the soul from the body. It is thus also possible on this theory that the early stage fetus has no soul, for it is not conscious and has no capacity for thinking.

THE SANCTITY OF LIFE
VIEW OF THE SOUL

The religious pro-life view of the soul agrees with, and is supported by, some of the ideas of Aristotle and some of the ideas of Descartes, but it is inconsistent with other parts of each view. With Aristotle, the sanctity of life view agrees that the soul is what makes a human being alive and is present from the moment of conception to the moment all life signs cease. Those who hold this view, however, disagree with Aristotle's view that the soul is not a substance but merely a cluster of properties, and, more important, they disagree with the idea that animals and plants have souls and that having a soul does not make humans morally special in any way. (For Aristotle, humans are morally special, but it is not merely because they have a soul. It is because of certain capacities unique to us.) The sanctity of life view agrees with Descartes that the soul is a substance and that it is what gives humans a special moral status. What they disagree with is the idea that the soul is not essential to life. They disagree with the claim that a fetus or brain-dead person might not have a soul.

By looking at what holders of the sanctity of life view agree with and disagree with from these two very different philosophical theories about the soul, we can piece together a fairly complete conception of the soul that must be affirmed by those who accept the sanctity of life principle, if it is to be internally coherent. I will call this view *substantive vitalism*. I do not mean to claim that all religious people (or even all people who disapprove of abortion on religious grounds) have this view of the soul. All I am claiming is that this is the view of the soul that many religious pro-lifers have, or seem to have. I do not want to saddle anyone with a position they do not ascribe to. I accept that I may be mistaken and may be misrepresenting the views of those who accept the sanctity of life principle. But any mischaracterization of their views is accidental. I am going to try to present the strongest, most plausible conception of the soul that could ground the strict pro-life position (sanctity of life). If my characterization is inaccurate, I invite anyone to present me with a theory of the soul that more accurately represents the beliefs of those who claim that the soul makes all human life sacred.

With these qualifications and disclaimers out of the way, let's look at this theory of the soul that we have dubbed substantive vitalism.

1. The soul is a substance (it can exist on its own, separate from the body).
2. The soul is nonphysical.
3. The soul is identical with the self or the essential part of who each person is.
4. The soul is what gives humans special moral status. (And since only humans have a soul, only humans have this special moral status.)
5. The soul is what makes a human being alive, and so all living humans have a soul from the very beginning (conception) to the very end (biological death).

Most Christians would probably make other important claims about the soul: it is immortal, it is created by God, and so on. I will not include these other considerations since they have theological rather than moral implications. But anyone who accepts this conception of the soul may feel free to add them if they wish.

NATURALISM AND THE HUMAN PERSON

Having considered the religious pro-life view of the human person, which consists of a body and a substantive soul that makes it alive, we should consider the view of the human person held by those with a more naturalistic view of what it is to be alive. There are some people who accept neither the substantive vitalist conception of the soul nor the naturalistic view of the human person. There may be, for example, some Christian idealists who do not believe that the body exists but that it is only an illusion. (The Christian Scientists seem to be some sort of idealists.) These two views, substantive vitalism and the naturalistic view, seem to be the two dominant conceptions today among nonphilosophers of what a human being is. They are commonly held among those on opposite ends of the abortion debate.

It is most important, first of all, to avoid mischaracterizing the naturalist view. In any endeavor to foster discussion we must avoid presenting an obscene caricature of the view at hand. I have tried to present the religious pro-life position in a fair and accurate way, and now I must in fairness do the same with the naturalist view. We must also not give too narrow a characterization. It is certainly true that some people who have a naturalist view of the world see the human person as nothing more than a highly sophisticated biological machine, different from other machines only in that it evolved naturally rather than being designed and is made of organic tissue rather than gears, pulleys, and wires. This might even be what some people mean when they describe someone as being a "naturalist" in the strict sense. We, however, are going to use "naturalist" to refer simply to someone who has a naturalistic view about life or what it is to be alive. It thus refers to ordinary, commonsense views about being alive that are scientific rather than religious or supernatural. By "scientific" I mean to include psychology and the social sciences, not just biology, chemistry, and the natural sciences. Such a view need not exclude beliefs in the existence of a God, but naturalists will give preference to natural explanations for ordinary objects and events rather than to supernatural ones. Most important for our discussion, they are going to support their moral claims by giving reasons in natural, observable terms rather than by appealing to something supernatural, such as God or a nonphysical soul. These people need not be entirely atheists. They may believe in God and the soul. But, if they believe in the soul, they will have a view of the soul that differs significantly from substantive vitalism.

The body is the biological organism explained by natural laws and able to be understood entirely within the science of biology. On this view, being alive consists of a cluster of chemical and physiological processes that sustain the organism. For the human body, these include breathing, circulation of the blood (heartbeat), cell division, digestion, neuron firings, and so on. These are roughly the processes that Aristotle identified as the basic powers of the soul common to all living things. Being biologically alive is, according to the naturalistic account, a natural, observable phenomenon, not a supernatural phenomenon. That is the essence of the naturalist view of life.

Because life is a cluster of processes, it may be hard to determine exactly when a person dies. This is not merely a practical difficulty but a theoretical difficulty. If the heart is not beating but the cells are still alive, being oxygenated by artificial means, then is the person still alive? On the substantive vitalism view, there is a clear answer to this question: if the soul is still present, then the person is still alive; if not, then the person is dead. We may not *know* exactly when this occurs, but it is, according to substantive vitalism, a real event and marks the true death of the person. Being alive or dead is an all-or-nothing deal. For the naturalist, there is a gray area of being semialive (though *most* people are either all-the-way alive or all-the-way dead). For substantive vitalism, dying is like flicking off a light switch. For the naturalists, it can be more like turning a dimmer all the way down (which sometimes happens very quickly, sometimes more gradually).

This, however, is only a part of what life is for the naturalist. There are two distinct senses in which someone is alive or dead. There is being alive in the strictly biological sense, and there is also being alive in a psychological sense, as a person. The life of the physical body is the primary sense in which we say someone is alive or dead; being mentally alive is another distinct sense.

Philosophers make a distinction between what they refer to as a "human being" and what they refer to as a "person." Though these terms are often used interchangeably in ordinary discourse, we will use them to refer to two different categories of things. A *human* is a biological entity, a living organism of the species *Homo sapiens sapiens*. A *person*, on the other hand, is a being with certain mental or psychological capacities. There is considerable debate among philosophers as to what exactly constitutes being a person. Some say it is the capacity for rational thought, others say the capacity for human emotions; still others say a certain kind of self-consciousness. (A philosopher named Mary Ann Warren has written a very good paper on this issue.) Though it is a matter of philosophical debate as to exactly what properties count as being a person and where to draw the line, most naturalists would agree that someone with none of these properties, someone who has lost all consciousness permanently or has never acquired these properties, is not a person (although she might still be *human*, that is, biologically alive and of the human species). Thus someone who is brain-dead is no longer a person, nor is an early stage embryo quite yet a person. Someone could also be a person without being human, at least theoretically. *Star Trek*'s Mr. Spock, for example, is a person. He has all of those qualities that we think of as being essential to personhood. But he is a Vulcan, not a human.

The question under debate is "What is it that makes someone have moral significance?" Is it being a member of the human species? That is not very plausible, for then we would owe Spock no moral consideration—or at least no more than we owe to other nonhuman animals, like cows or pigs. Or is it the possession of a soul that gives a being special moral worth? This seems more likely, especially if we also claim that having a soul is necessary to have those other properties, and that Spock must have a soul like ours, even though he is not human. The substantive vitalists hold this view, but they also

hold the view that one can still have a soul even without having these properties of personhood. The third possibility is that it is being a person that
gives one special moral status. The naturalist holds this view. And many naturalists think that these properties do not require a soul—at least not of the
substantive vitalist sort.

Although many of those whom we are calling naturalists believe that
these mental or psychological capacities are merely activities of the brain,
some of those included in this group might believe that these capacities are
somehow related to some nonphysical mind or soul that is distinct from the
body. What unites these divergent views into the broad category of naturalist
is that for all of them, being *biologically* alive is a natural, physical property
or set of properties. The presence of some supernatural entity or force is not
needed for a human being to be *biologically* alive, nor is it needed to explain
biological life. It is this that puts these believers into the same group as the
atheists who dismiss the soul as pure nonsense, and it is this that separates
them from their fellow believers who see being biologically alive as
requiring a supernatural explanation. This difference is also at least one of
the things that makes any debate impossible. Even those naturalists who feel
that abortion is morally wrong are not necessarily going to be in agreement
with substantial vitalism, for they will oppose abortion for different reasons
and are not necessarily committed to the sanctity of life.

It goes without saying, perhaps, that for the naturalist—whether atheist
or believer—what is of greatest moral significance and what makes people
morally special are primarily those mental or psychological capacities that
make a mere human being a person. Of course, those who hold the substantive vitalism view and those who are naturalists will both be inclined to think
that we have some duties to nonpersons such as nonhuman animals, even if
they are lesser duties. Both sides can probably agree that torturing animals
for pleasure is morally wrong, for example. They might even agree for some
of the same reasons. The same goes for dead humans. Although both would
agree that they do not have the same moral status as living people, there are
presumably some things that it would be wrong to do to a human corpse,
such as necrophilia or posing it in degrading positions for one's own amuse-
ment. The essential difference between the two views comes in those examples of human beings that are still alive but are no longer persons. For
substantive vitalism, as long as there is a heartbeat, even an artificially stim-
ulated one, there is still a soul and thus such a human being has basically the

same right to live as you or I have. That is the sanctity of life position. For the naturalist, such a brain-dead human being is no longer a person and so no longer has the same rights as you or I have. We may still have some moral obligations to this being as we do to animals or human corpses, but it does not belong to the same class, morally speaking, as do full-fledged persons.

SUGGESTED FURTHER READING

Warren, Mary Ann. "On the Moral and Legal Status of Abortion." *Monist* 57 (January 1973): 43–61.

CHAPTER 3

LIFE BEGINS AT CONCEPTION— SO WHAT?

EQUIVOCATION

One of the most common confusions and mistakes in reasoning, especially in reasoning about difficult and controversial topics like abortion, is a logical error known as *equivocation*. An equivocation is when we have a term that has two or more distinct meanings that become confused, or when we switch between the two meanings while treating the term as if it had one, univocal meaning. For example, consider the following:

(1) Children should not have to work for a living.
(2) I am my mother's child.
(3) Therefore, I should not have to work for a living.

Of course, this example is comical because the equivocation is so obvious that no one would be fooled or confused by it. I use the obviousness of this example to show that any argument based on an equivocation is a very weak argument or no argument at all. The argument proves nothing because the term child means something very different in its two uses in the argument. In the first claim (that children should not have to earn a wage) we use the term child to mean a *minor* (or, as they say down here in southern Mississippi, a *young'n'*). In the second claim (that I am someone's child) we mean child in the sense of *offspring*. So if we clarify our argument by substituting the term child with more precise terms, we eliminate the equivocation. What we end up with is something like this:

(1) Minors should not have to work for a living.
(2) I am my mother's offspring.

Now it is obvious that nothing follows from these two claims, whether or not they are true. They are completely unrelated to each other.

Understanding what equivocation is, and appreciating how and why arguments guilty of equivocating on some crucial term prove nothing, will help us avoid a common mistake in the abortion debate. This will help us to clarify exactly what the substantive vitalists and the naturalists agree on and, equally important, what they do not agree on. Then we can see what follows (and what does not follow) from their claims.

THE MEANING OF "LIFE"

"Life begins at conception." This is a phrase often uttered by those who support the sanctity of life principle and try to win the argument without doing any real work. They think that all they need to do is to establish this claim, and from there it would follow that abortion is morally wrong at any stage in fetal development. We must look past the rhetoric of the "life begins at conception" slogan. It often causes embarrassment to the pro-choicer who is at a loss to respond, since it seems absurd to deny that the fertilized egg is not alive. This embarrassment, however, in entirely unwarranted. The pro-choice side can accept the slogan without conceding anything important in the debate. Life does begin at conception. But of course, we cannot infer anything about the morality of abortion from this one statement alone. We need to add another claim, that it is wrong to take an innocent human life. This claim is one that is assumed in the argument, and those who accept the naturalist view of life would probably agree to it. But the claim that abortion is wrong does not necessarily follow from these two claims. What we need in order to clear up the confusion and disagreement is to demand a clear definition of the term *life*.

The naturalist might agree that life begins at conception, but only as long as "life" means nothing more than the state of being *biologically* alive. This sense of "life," for the naturalist, refers to the biochemical processes that constitute nutrition, reproduction, growth, and so on. The naturalist does not think that being biologically alive gives something any special moral status; certainly not the same moral status as you and I have. Life may begin at conception, but animals and plants and even microorganisms are all alive. The pro-lifer may insist that the freshly conceived zygote is a living *human* being, and that it is the combination of being alive and being human that gives it special moral status. Again, this should cause no embarrassment to the pro-choicer. Someone with a naturalist view of life would demand a clear definition of "human." The zygote is human in the sense of belonging to the human species rather than to some other species. (It is a *human* zygote rather than an *elephant* zygote or a *turtle* zygote, etc.) But it is not yet a human specimen in the sense that it does not yet have the standard human anatomy. It is not even a vertebrate in that it does not yet have a spine. And it is certainly not a person.

Thus there are two senses of being alive. One sense is the purely biological sense. The other sense still needs to be defined. For the substantive vitalist this would be the possession of a soul; for the naturalist it would be whatever qualities make one a person.

POTENTIAL PERSON

Obviously there is something very different from a fertilized human egg cell and some single-celled protozoan. The human zygote is a potential person who will develop into someone like you or me. The appeal to potential personhood is popular among professional philosophers with their esoteric metaphysical concepts and their bizarre thought experiments. It is also a popular argument among nonphilosophers. Thus I will discuss these ideas in chapter 6. At this point, however, we should stick to the debate between the naturalist view of life and substantive vitalism. The potential person debate does not divide evenly between these two views. Many naturalists think that the potential for being a person is enough to grant the fetus full moral status. For this reason, not all naturalists are pro-choice. But of course, it still would not support the sanctity of life principle because those who are brain-dead no longer have any potential for ever being a person. Even on the other side, some substantive vitalists believe that potential for personhood is another argument against abortion, while some might think that it is irrelevant and that if it had potential for being a person but had no soul (at least not yet), then it would not be wrong to kill it.

THE CONCEPT OF CONCEPTION

Both sides can agree that life begins at conception (though by this we mean only biological life). They disagree, however, about what constitutes this biological life. The substantive vitalist believes that biological life, at least for humans, requires a supernatural soul and that this gives the fetus special moral status, while the naturalist either rejects the notion of the soul altogether or identifies the soul with consciousness or rationality, which are not present at conception. According to the naturalist, mere biological life, which is nothing more than a complex set of biochemical processes, does not grant the living human being with any special moral status—or at least not with a status comparable to that of a fully developed person like you or me.

The fact that both sides can agree that biological life begins at conception is no small matter, for it indicates something important that both sides can accept. This might provide a place to compare their competing notions of life. Why is this one simple point of agreement so useful? Because it is *not* just one simple point. To agree that life begins at conception requires agreement on a great number of things, an entire theory composed of explanations, causal connections, and observable facts. Agreeing that biological life begins at conception indicates that they both agree, for the most part at least, on the biological theory of reproduction. That is quite a large agreement.

It should be expected that the naturalist accepts the scientific theory of human reproduction; after all, the naturalists are the ones with the more scientifically minded view of the world (at least when it comes to life). But if the substantive vitalists claim that life begins at conception, then they must agree as well, for the very notion of "conception" is a biological concept, part of the scientific theory of reproduction. Presumably, when the religious pro-lifer says life begins at conception, by the term "conception" he means when the sperm meets the egg.

So both naturalists and substantive vitalists believe that a human being's biological life begins when a man's sperm cell meets up with a woman's egg cell, each sharing their half set of DNA to make one complete set. This normally occurs in the woman's uterus and is usually the result of sexual inter-course—but it could also take place in a petri dish. This fertilized egg then spontaneously begins to develop into a fetus (and into a placenta), implants itself into the woman's uterine lining, and, with nutrients and oxygen sup-plied by the woman's blood, grows into a fully developed human infant. After about nine and a half months, when it is ready to come out of the oven, so to speak, the baby is born. This is very important because if both sides did not agree on where babies come from, then we could not adequately com-pare their competing claims about the moral status of the fetus. If they held different theories, then we could look only at how the naturalist's view of the fetus fits into the naturalist theory of reproduction and how the substantive vitalist's view of the fetus fits in with the substantive vitalist's theory of reproduction. We might also be able to try to determine which theory of re-production is better, but this would be difficult because we would not have a common ground from which to assess them both fairly. If we critique one of the theories, the proponents of that theory could question the grounds from which we are critiquing it. This is why it is of great significance that each side agree on the scientific theory of reproduction.

Suppose, for example, that the pro-lifer rejected the standard scientific theory of human reproduction in favor of some alternative theory, such as the cabbage patch theory (which is clearly superior to the absurd stork theory!). In that case we could not all agree that biological life begins at conception. The naturalist would insist that biological life begins when the sperm cell fertilizes the egg cell, while the pro-lifer would insist that biological life begins when the cabbage plant first begins to sprout. Although both might refer to this beginning event as "conception," they would be equivocating on the term and thus not agreeing at all on how or when life begins. Fortunately, since both naturalists and substantive vitalists agree on the standard theory of human reproduction, we can look at how each of these theories fits within that picture.

HOME FIELD ADVANTAGE FOR THE NATURALIST?

The substantive vitalists need not worry that they are fighting on foreign ground or that the biological theory of reproduction automatically guarantees victory to the naturalist. It is true that the science of biology tries to explain human reproduction purely through the mechanism of cause and effect as the interaction of physical and chemical substances according to laws of nature. The biologist excludes from the explanation any mention of the nonphysical or supernatural. That is just a part of doing good science. But to exclude the nonphysical soul from any part of scientific discussion is not to prove that it does not exist. (On the contrary, to argue that it does not exist would require discussing it.) To even mention something that is not part of the observable world, beyond the physical realm, is to go outside of the domain of science and into the domain of religion (or philosophy). Many biologists believe in something beyond the natural world, but if they try to make *scientific* assertions about nonphysical or spiritual things, then they are doing bad *science* (or not doing science at all).

This is not to assert the dominance of science but, on the contrary, to proscribe the *boundary* of science. Some things lie outside of its inquiry. To insist, or even to allow, science to make determinations about supernatural matters would be analogous to using mathematics or geometry to determine what is morally right. Moral concepts are not allowed in mathematics, but that does not mean that mathematicians cannot have moral beliefs. It just means that these beliefs are not mathematical. Science excludes nonphysical entities because it is only the study of observable entities and events; and scientists try to give a minimal explanation, one that includes as few principles or entities as needed. This is not to say that there is nothing outside of the physical observable world but only that if there is, it has no place in science. The religious pro-lifer can accept the biological facts but then say that there is something beyond them. Naturalists, on the other hand, claim that science gives us a complete explanation (or at least a complete explanation of what it is to be biologically alive).

If pro-lifers are still not happy discussing the matter in terms of the standard scientific theory of reproduction, then they must be able to come up with a reasonable alternative theory. There have been rival theories in the past. The protoscientific alchemists believed that the potential person was a *homunculus*, or "little man," that lived inside the sperm. The woman's womb, on this view, provides only the nourishing environment—the fertile soil, as it were—into which the man sows his "seed." On this view, the biological life of a particular human begins much earlier than in our current understanding. The fetus is already developing in the father's testicles. There are obvious problems with view, such as its inability to explain why children resemble their mothers. But more important, this view is incompatible with the pro-lifers' claim that life starts at conception, for on this view there is no conception, at least not as the word conception is commonly defined to mean the uniting of a sperm and an egg cell. Adherents to the homuncular theory, then, would have to pinpoint some other event as the moment during which life begins. And if life begins during spermatogenesis, then masturbating to orgasm, or even having sex with the intent of inducing pregnancy, would involve the destruction of millions of potential persons. If that were true, then it seems that male masturbation would be much worse than an abortion, which ends only the life of *one* potential person. In order for pro-lifers to maintain their claim that "life begins at conception" they must either accept the standard theory of reproduction or present an alternative theory that preserves the meaning of the term conception to mean the uniting of a sperm cell and egg cell.

A LITTLE BIOLOGY

So what is the basic theory of human reproduction and development that both sides agree on? It is the basic story told in any high school textbook on the subject. Since it may have been a while since some of my readers have taken high school biology, we should remind ourselves of the details of this story.

Every normal human being has 46 chromosomes grouped into 23 pairs. If human reproductive cells (sperm and eggs) had the full set of chromosomes, then the resulting offspring would have double the full set: four sets of 23 for a grand total of 92 chromosomes. In the real world of biology such a fetus would not be viable; it would die in the womb and be spontaneously aborted. But if it were viable, if this were the way that reproduction worked, then the chromosomes of each successive generation would be twice that of the previous generation. After just a dozen or so generations the DNA of one cell would weigh several hundred pounds and take up more volume than a fully grown human being. This would not be very practical. To avoid this absurdity, nature has devised a simple solution. The reproductive cells, or *gametes*, contain only 23 individual chromosomes—one from each pair, selected randomly. Thus when the sperm fertilizes the egg at conception, the resulting zygote will have the normal 46 chromosomes, 23 pairs with each pair consisting of one chromosome from the woman and one chromosome from the man.

There is another advantage of this system. The offspring inherits only half of its father's DNA and only half of its mother's DNA. This makes it possible for certain characteristics to be selected for or against. If the father has some bad gene on one of his chromosomes, then each child has only a 50 percent chance of inheriting that gene. If each gamete had all of the chromosomes of each parent, then every offspring would inherit the bad gene. So in the formation of the gametes (egg and sperm cells) the DNA in the nucleus of the cells multiplies to make two identical copies of all 46 chromosomes, but instead of dividing once (as with normal cell division), it divides once and then both cells divide again. The two sets of 46 chromosomes are divided among four cells, giving each 23 chromosomes—half of the complete set.

CONCEPTION

Conception takes place when the sperm cell hooks up with the egg cell and deposits its genetic material inside the wall of the egg cell. To be technically accurate, the sperm does not enter an egg cell with 23 chromosomes. When the sperm first breaches its cell wall, the ovum has not yet finished the process of meiosis—it has undergone only the first of the two divisions, so it has the full set of 46 chromosomes. Only after the sperm enters the ovum does it bother to divide the final time, thereby reducing its genetic material to the 23 individual chromosomes. Only then can the DNA of the sperm combine with the DNA of the egg, forming a complete set of 46 chromosomes in 23 pairs, each pair containing one chromosome from the man's sperm and one chromosome from the woman's egg.

The fertilized egg, called a *zygote*, then slowly but gradually starts to develop. The first thing it does is merely divide into two cells. Since human beings are very complex organisms composed of many different kinds of highly specialized cells, dividing from one into two is all that the zygote can do at first. Dividing from two into four is all that it can do next. Specialized cells are a long way off, let alone specific parts or discrete organs. Many other things, and much more dividing, must happen first.

This cell division takes place very slowly. It takes about twelve hours for the DNA from the sperm to fuse with the DNA of the egg and about eighteen hours more for the first cell division to take place. The dividing begins slowly because it starts off as one lone cell. The pace of development increases rapidly—not because the cells divide faster but because there are more of them, all dividing at the same time. After a week there are only about 200 or so cells. At this point the cells have no structure, no particular arrangement. They are just a blob of undifferentiated cells. These are so-called stem cells—cells that have not yet specialized into any particular kind of cell. They are special and have great potential for medical use, because a stem cell can become any kind of cell: bone cell, muscle cell, brain cell, skin cell, nerve cell, and so on.

This blob of cells, called a *blastocyst*, eventually begins to organize itself and form structures. What structures come first? Certainly not any particular human parts like a heart or a brain or a spleen. There is not even an inside/outside division of the fetus. No, the first structures to develop are not going to be part of the fetus at all (or at least not part of the future person). The first form that the blastocyst takes is that of a hollow sphere. Most of this sphere will develop not into part of the fetus but into placenta—the temporary organ that surrounds the developing fetus and sucks up nutrients and oxygen from the mother's blood, which is then delivered to the fetus through the umbilical cord and exchanged with its own waste. (The inside half of the placenta is formed by the fetus, the half outside of that is formed by the mother's uterus. Where the fetal half meets the mother's half is the placental barrier.) It is important to note that most of the support structures for the fetus—the umbilical cord, the amniotic sac, and the inside of the placenta—are all provided by the developing embryo, not by the mother's body, which is comparatively passive, at least in the earlier stages.

At this early stage, the embryo is not yet embedded into the uterus but is free-floating, unconnected to the mother except indirectly through hormonal messages and a few stray nutrients. This is why the placenta forms first. The fetus cannot grow without food. In fact, for all of its cell dividing the fetus has not gotten much larger at this stage; each division results in smaller and smaller cells. So the first task is to embed itself into the lining of the uterus where it will burst open the mother's blood vessels and absorb the goodness (nutrients and oxygen) from her spilt blood.

The fetus itself, or, rather, what will become the fetus, is at this point merely a slightly thicker mass of cells on one side of this hollow ball. Eventually (after implantation) this thin sheet of cells separates off from the side, dividing the inside of the blastocyst into two chambers. The new chamber is the *amniosis*, which will gradually expand to surround the entire fetus. The original chamber, called the *yoke sac*, will eventually become the inside of the fetus (and its umbilical cord) once the disk that is to form the fetus folds over and pinches off this area. When it first separates from the edge, the fetal disk is only a translucent film two cells thick. The layer closest to the yoke will become the inside part of the body—the intestinal tract, the lungs, and a few other organs. The other layer will form the outside; from it will develop the skin, muscles, bones, and many other important organs. At this point, however, it is all undifferentiated and without structure. It is just a disk, and the cells are all of the same unspecialized type.

It is only after two weeks or so that the embryo starts to take on meaningful shape and develop specialized tissues. This takes place through an elaborate sequence of folding and refolding—like some organic origami—to create insides and outsides. The first such folding starts with a groove forming across the disk. This groove is then filled with cells that will develop into nerve cells and eventually develop into the spine and nervous system. Then the groove seals itself back up. The next folding involves the formation of a cavity where the brain will form. The embryo is still a disk, but now it has an axis (the spine) and that axis has a head end and a tail end. Next, the biggest folding takes place, which transforms the disk into more of a tube-like shape, curved and sealed off at both ends. The disk is never separate from the rest of the blastocyst (which is forming into the placenta), but where the fold comes together it forms the umbilical cord. After three weeks small bumps appear on the tubelike torso. These bumps will grow into arms and legs.

It is interesting to note that all embryos, whether they have XX or XY sex chromosomes, start out developing into females. It is only the interference of this process by hormones produced by the Y chromosome that steers the embryo away from its normal female development and diverts it toward the male direction. Thus it is incorrect to think of the X chromosome as a sex chromosome. Only the Y chromosome determines sex; with it the fetus becomes a male, without it, a female. If a fetus had neither X nor Y, it would develop into a female, though an unviable one.

REPRODUCTION AND SUBSTANTIVE VITALISM

We might want to question at this point whether the sanctity of life position (along with substantive vitalism) is coherent. The theory holds that life begins at conception, and from that very moment we have a human being in the full sense (not merely a potential human being). The soul is present at the moment of conception, and at that very moment the entity thus has the same moral status as any other human being.

One issue that might be raised by opponents of this view is the problem of pinpointing the exact moment of conception. If life is an all-or-nothing matter, as substantive vitalists claim, then life must begin all at once at some instant in time. It could not happen gradually. The problem, however, is that conception does not occur in one instantaneous moment. It is a gradual process with many steps extended over several hours. Does life begin at the moment when the sperm first enters the egg? But at that moment there are sixty-nine chromosomes (three sets of twenty-three). Maybe we should consider conception to occur when the egg, simulated by the presence of the sperm, makes its final division, resulting in the normal 46 chromosomes. (Of course, sometimes the egg does not undergo the final division, and a fetus starts to develop with sixty-nine chromosomes—but it does not get very far. It is not viable. But is it alive according to the sanctity of life principle?) Maybe we should consider the beginning of life to be the point in time when the sperm DNA starts to mix and mingle with the egg DNA. Then why not insist that it is only when they have completely mingled?

This question of when exactly life begins may seem to be of little practical importance. Contraception (with the possible exception of the IUD) prohibits the sperm from coming anywhere near the egg cell, and so takes place well before anything else happens. Condoms and diaphragms prevent the sperm from getting into the uterus, while the pill prohibits the egg from entering the uterus. In either case, as long as contraception works, never the twain shall meet. And whenever abortion is performed by standard procedures available today, the fetus is well past any of this conception business. Even with the earliest abortion techniques—the abortion pill—the fertilized cell has already multiplied into hundreds of cells and has implanted itself into the woman's uterus. (The IUD works even earlier in the process; it prevents the blastocyst from implanting itself in the woman's uterus. This would still be well after conception.) Thus according to the sanctity of life view, any form of contraception (including the morning after pill) should be morally OK since it begins working before contraception, and, likewise, any abortion (as well as the IUD) would be wrong because it works after conception and so involves the taking of a human life.

However, the substantive vitalist cannot escape this problem of having to pinpoint the exact moment of conception by claiming that it is of no practical concern. Substantive vitalism is not merely a practical principle but a theoretical claim that serves as a basis for practical principles. It is simply a contingent fact that it is of no practical concern. It just so happens that all of the available forms of birth control operate well on one side or the other of conception. It *could* become a practical concern given new techniques or unusual scenarios. If substantive vitalism is going to ground moral principles, then it must also be able to guide us in those borderline cases.

Consider this possibility. Suppose biochemical engineers develop a new and highly effective birth control pill with no side effects. This new pill works very differently from our current progestin-based pills. It does not prevent ovulation, nor does it prevent sperm from entering into the uterus. It does not even prevent the sperm from entering into the egg cell. But as soon as the sperm cell passes the cell wall of the egg cell, this new drug prevents the dissolving of the cell wall of the sperm's head, thus preventing its DNA from intermingling with the DNA of the egg cell. Would this be contraception or abortion, according to substantive vitalism? If conception is the sperm entering the egg cell, then it would be equivalent to abortion. If contraception is the intermingling of the sperm-DNA with the egg-DNA, then it would be merely contraception (it would prevent conception and there would be no life at this point). The sanctity of life principle needs to be able to make this call, for it assumes that life is an all-or-nothing matter. But it is not obvious why we should prefer one cutoff point over the other.

It is important to avoid making the following mistake. We cannot start with our intuitions about whether it would be wrong to use this kind of birth control. Whether or not we should oppose it, according to the sanctity of life principle, depends on whether or not it is a living human being. To base the decision on our moral intuitions about this type of birth control would be to make the determination of whether or not something is a living human being depend on our attitudes toward it.

Of course, the pro-lifer can argue that we simply do not know and so we should err on the side of caution, drawing the conception line on the early side. This way we can be reasonably sure that we are not taking any human lives with our birth control methods. To do otherwise without a definitive answer for exactly where human life starts would be careless. This might be the best thing to do practically, given the uncertainty about what instant is *the* instant that conception takes place. But our question was not a practical one, it was theoretical. Substance vitalism is not merely a practical theory, it makes theoretical claims about when life—in the morally relevant sense—begins. Faced with this question of which of the series of events that constitutes conception is the one event where "it all happens," the substantive vitalist seems to be faced with one of two options. Either he must say that we don't know, in which case the theory cannot explain something that it is supposed to explain; or he must pick a moment arbitrarily, but he could give no reason why we should think life begins at that moment or at one of the other moments that constitute conception.

I do not think, however, that this problem is devastating for the substantive vitalist. For one, substantive vitalism is a theory of the soul and not a theory of biology. Even if it equates the soul with biological life, it is not meant as a substitute for biological science or medicine, and so it need not explain biological events or processes. Of course, since it equates biological life with the presence of the soul, it must be *consistent* with biological facts. But the theory does seem to be contradicted by the scientific biological theory of conception and human development. The substantive vitalist notion of the soul and the claim that life begins at one instant does not exclude the possibility that certain events must take place just before that moment, in preparation for it, or just after the life-giving event, in continuation of it. Also, the substantive vitalist can leave unanswered the question as to exactly when the event takes place. A good theory need not provide us with an answer to every possible question. And this is not even an answer internal to the theory but a question of how this theory (about the soul) maps onto a different theory (the biological theory of reproduction). Since substantive vitalists take this other theory to be more or less true, substantive vitalism must be consistent with it. However, I see no reason why the substantive vitalist needs to determine exactly how it links up at every point.

NATURALISM, CONCEPTION, AND THE BEGINNING OF LIFE

Since we have examined how substantive vitalism is related to the scientific theory of human reproduction, and with conception in particular, we should also take a moment to consider how the naturalist's view of the human being relates to this theory. The naturalist is probably more comfortable with the details of conception and human development, considering that her view is that life is the observable physical states and processes. Since the naturalist sees biological life as a cluster of properties and processes, it does not matter that life does not start all at once and completely. It starts at first only on the cellular level, and, at the earliest stages, it undergoes reproduction only in the form of multiplication of individual cells. At this very beginning the embryo, or blastocyst, does not undergo any growth or any of the nutritive processes. It does not yet have any organ for collecting nutrients and disposing of waste. So without any source of new building materials it does not get any bigger, even though it divides into hundreds of cells. Instead, each new cell is half the size of the cell it divided from—like cutting a pizza into smaller and smaller servings: there may be more slices, but it is still only a twelve-inch pie. This is why the first structures to develop are the placebo; the embryo needs to get food in order to grow.

SUGGESTED FURTHER READING

Zimmer, Carl. "Silent Struggle: A New Theory of Pregnancy." *New York Times*, March 14, 2006.

CHAPTER 4
ABNORMAL HUMAN DEVELOPMENT

B oth theories of what counts as being alive for a human being—the substantive vitalist view and the naturalist view—are coherent theories. Neither of them contains any obvious self-contradictory claims or any unbearable ambiguity or confusion. Thus both are, at this point at least, legitimate contenders in the philosophy ring for being the true theory. In the revealed theology ring, of course, substantive vitalism might have the decided edge. But it would be an unfair advantage, for the Bible was not intended to be the final authority on everything—math and science as much as God and salvation. Certainly we would not want to replace medical textbooks with Bibles to train our future physicians. If the contest were held in biology classrooms and laboratories, on the other hand, that would provide an easy victory for the naturalists. But again, it would be an undeserved victory. Biology must define life strictly in terms of observable, measurable phenomena in order to study it scientifically. But the question "What is life?" is not itself a question about what we can observe or measure. We are not asking how Christian theologians must define it or how biologists must define it; we are asking which definition fits with reality. This is a question that can only be asked outside these fields, in a neutral zone with no commitments to any particular method, domain of entities, or picture of the world. In other words, we must ask this question on the neutral playing field of philosophy.

How do we judge which of these two views is superior philosophically? First we can look for any inconsistency within each theory. This would be an internal analysis. If there is none, then we must examine how each theory fits with other things we know or strongly believe. If one theory is inconsistent with other things we have good reason to believe, then that is a strike against the theory. How telling a blow it is against the theory will depend on how good are the reasons for maintaining those other beliefs and how much we would lose if we abandoned them.

So in order to assess vitalism and naturalism, we must see how each one fits with the rest of our knowledge. To do this fairly, without biasing one view over the other, we must see how it compares with beliefs that are accepted by both parties. We could not test naturalism, for example, on the basis of how it fits with what the Bible says, because the naturalist is not going to accept the Bible as the literal truth about what life is. Likewise we could not contrast vitalism with the theory of evolution because the vitalist might not think that life can be reduced to biological processes.

In the previous chapter we started to test the respective theories to other things we know when we compared both theories to our beliefs about human reproduction and embryonic development. Our results were not decisive. Although vitalism could not pinpoint exactly which biological moment of the conception process coincided with the metaphysical event of the soul coming to be present, this does not constitute any inconsistency in the theory itself.

Now I propose that we look at how each of these theories maps onto what we know about abnormal human reproduction and development. The reason for this approach is this: The theories under consideration are theories about what makes any human being alive, not just about most human beings. They are theories of what constitutes human life itself, not simply typical human life. Thus they should apply to abnormal cases as well as normal cases. This is a common strategy in testing any theory, scientific or philosophical. It is usually not so hard to get a theory to work for normal cases; it is harder to find a theory that adequately deals with unusual cases as well as normal cases. Let me give an example to illustrate this point.

Newtonian physics works well enough for most calculations about the movements of physical objects through space. It was even good enough for all of the calculations needed to land astronauts on the Moon and bring them back safely to Earth. However, when we try to apply Newtonian physics to supermassive objects or to tiny subatomic particles moving at speeds approaching the speed of light, then everything breaks down. Newton's theory works perfectly well for mundane objects like spaceships and planets, but for those objects that are not part of normal experience (black holes, electrons, etc.), we need to apply Einstein's theory of relativity.

Insofar as vitalism and the naturalist theory of life are both theories about what makes a human being biologically alive—and adherents of both theories will agree on the facts about abnormal human development—then we should compare each theory with these facts. If one theory is inconsistent with the facts, then we should consider rejecting it (depending on how committed we are to these facts). Of course, it is possible that both theories will turn out to contradict the facts. In that case we should reject them both in favor of some third alternative theory that can peacefully coexist with what we know about human reproduction and development. There may be other theories about what makes a human being alive that are significantly different from both of these views. Thus rejecting one of these theories does not automatically mean we should accept the other theory.

Though one theory (or both) might be inconsistent with the facts, it is more likely that neither will be flatly contradicted by what we know about human life and reproduction. It is probable, however, that even if both theories are logically consistent with the facts, one of them is a better fit. All other things being equal, we should prefer the theory that better maps onto these facts, since the theories are supposed to describe what these facts consist of.

E UNUM, PLURIBUS

The first type of abnormal human development we must consider is that of identical twins. One might be surprised that identical twins would be considered abnormal. But by "abnormal" I do not mean to imply that they are unhealthy or unfortunate. I simply mean *not normal*, in other words, atypical. Identical twins deviate from the norm in that most of the time a fertilized egg results in one and only one fetus. Of course, nonidentical twins are also abnormal in this sense. But nonidentical twins will not serve as a helpful example because each of the nonidentical twins is conceived and develops in the normal, textbook way. From start to finish each originates from one egg fertilized by one sperm resulting in one human being. Identical twins, however, are another matter altogether.

Let's start with a brief sketch of how identical twins develop. Identical twins start out as one egg cell fertilized by a single sperm. The resulting zygote then multiplies and starts to develop like any other human embryo. Then at some point, for whatever reason, the cluster of cells that would normally develop into a human being divides into two clusters of cells, each of which will develop into a different human being (and eventually into two distinct persons). The embryo starts off as one human being (or potential human being) and then splits off into two (potential) human beings. Since each of these two come from the same zygote—the same one egg fertilized by the same one sperm—each of the twins will have the exact same genetic material.

The question we must now ask is how each of the theories being considered fits with the phenomenon of identical twins. Though this may be a biological phenomenon, it does not give unfair advantage to the naturalist theory because, for one, adherents to vitalism cannot reasonably deny the existence of identical twins or the fact that they originate from a single fertilized egg. Furthermore, the existence of identical twins is not unique to the modern scientific biological theory but is part of the ordinary, commonly observable phenomena of everyday life. The identical twin is not a theoretical entity, which is posited in order to explain certain phenomena. It is one of the phenomena that the theory is supposed to explain. By analogy, the sun and the stars are observable objects that our theory of physics is intended to explain. Atoms, on the other hand, are purely theoretical entities. We cannot observe atoms themselves, but the idea of the atom was posited to explain other things that we can observe. Identical twins were known to exist well before, and independently of, the discovery of DNA, the theory of evolution, and any of the other essential elements of modern biology. Even if we reject modern biological theories, we still must admit that there are identical twins that start off as one and split into two.

So how does this fit with the vitalist view of the soul? Well, certainly the twins are two separate people and so each must have her own separate soul (or "Life"). This is obvious, since if one identical twin dies, the other can continue to live. The vitalist, however, claims that life begins at conception. At conception, and for several days after that, there is only one zygote (or blastocyst)—one cell or clump of cells. If it eventually becomes two people and if life begins at conception (and both of the twins' lives began at conception), then it must have had two souls at conception. That does not seem very reasonable. Another possibility is that at the time of division a new soul came into being. Of course, then vitalism would have to say that *either* life begins at conception *or*, if you are an identical twin, then maybe it begins several days later at the moment of dividing.

Then the vitalist is faced with the awkward question of which twin gets to keep the old soul and which gets the new one. There seems to be no reason why it should go one way rather than the other. The embryo divides right down the middle into two identical ones, each with the same number of cells. It is not as if one split off from the other through some kind of budding. Likewise, we can't try to solve this by asking which of the cells is the original fertilized cell, for when the zygote first divides, it also divides right down the middle into two new cells, each of which is half of the original cell. The answer to the question "Which one of the cells is the original?" is *all of them* (or none of them) equally. So which half gets the old soul and which gets the new one would have to be determined randomly or decided by divine fiat (which involves too much micromanaging for a deity to be expected to do) or by some arbitrary causal mechanism. At any rate there is an odd asymmetry here. One twin would have been alive for longer than the other, even though the cells are all equally old. Another possibility is that the soul itself divides, but that seems even more implausible than the other alternatives.

How, then, does the naturalist view of human life map onto the case of identical twins? Well, for the naturalist, the human being is a biological organism and as such is constituted by the cells that make up its body. Being alive is a cluster of physical processes performed by the cells and organs that make up the body. For the naturalist, being alive does not depend on any *other* thing that the embryo possesses. Thus, since the cluster of cells (and nothing more) is the living human being, when the cluster divides into two, then the embryo is also divided into two (potential) human beings. There is no further entity that constitutes, or is necessary for, biological life. Thus no other division or addition need be posited.

NOT QUITE TWO FROM ONE

Let us now consider another form of abnormal human reproduction and development that is closely related to normal identical twins—that of conjoined twins. Conjoined twins are identical twins who never quite separated all the way. Sometimes the twins are hardly connected at all. Chang and Eng, the famous nineteenth-century conjoined twins from Indochina (from whence we get the expression "Siamese twins") were connected only by skin, cartilage, and a liver. It would have been easy to separate them surgically, even back then. They were an example of *omphalopagus* conjoined twins. (*Pagus* means attached together; *omphalo* means belly or navel.) Another example of mostly separate conjoined twins is that of *craniopagus* twins (attached at the cranium). These twins are connected at the head, usually at the top of the head, but they have separate brains. These twins can also be separated, but the surgery is understandably quite delicate. On the other hand, some conjoined twins, such as *thoracopagus* (connected at the thorax, or torso) twins are connected at the chest and share most or even all of their vital organs, having only one heart, one liver, one pancreas, and so on between them.

At first it seems that the phenomenon of conjoined twins presents no further problems for the vitalist than the mildly irritating problems presented by the comparatively mundane phenomenon of identical twins. When we consider mostly separate twins like our friends Chang and Eng, we understand that they are clearly two distinct persons. They could be easily cleft from each other with only a minor operation, and they would not be significantly transformed (at least not biologically) by the separation. Certainly we would not say that there was one soul between them before they were separated and that there were two souls only after we severed the thin band that connected them. If they could be separated, it is clear that they would have two different souls (according to vitalism). And since they are virtually the same before the separation—except for the incidental fact that they are connected by a band of tissue—they must also have two souls before they are separated.

But now let us consider a case of more closely conjoined twins, such as thoracopagus twins, or the even more highly conjoined *dicephalic* ("two-headed") twins. Abby and Brittany Hensel are famous dicephalic twins, sharing one body except for their separate necks and heads. (Each has her own spine and stomach, and they share a third lung, but none of that is obvious from the outside.) These twins clearly cannot both live separately. If they were to be separated, then the one without the rest of the body would have zero chance of survival, even for a short time, and would die immediately. If having a soul constitutes (or is the essential cause of) being alive, as vitalism claims, then it is hard to see how Abby and Brittany could have more than one soul. They have only one biological life between them—one life that they could both share or one that could be lived by only one of them after an elaborate (and rather unethical) operation. Still, they are obviously two distinct persons. Thus they should be thought to have two distinct souls, if the soul is thought to be essential to personhood. But if there are two souls, then there is not a one-to-one correspondence between embodied human souls and (biologically) living human beings.

The problem is that substantive vitalism equates having a soul with being biologically alive, whereas the naturalist either denies that the soul exists or equates having a soul with something else, such as being a person. The highly conjoined twins seem to constitute two persons sharing one biological life.

Now consider a different, converse case of highly conjoined twins. *Cephalopagus* conjoined twins have only one head but can have two otherwise complete bodies. Each body has its own heart, its own liver, its own pair of kidneys, its own pair of lungs, and so on. Each has two arms and two legs, but only one head with one brain. Would such twins have two souls? This cephalopagus set of twins seems to be one person (or would be one person if the twins could survive long enough to become a person) with two bodies. Thus it seems like the set of twins should have only one soul. I see no serious moral problems with cutting off one of the bodies, even though it will die, to save the head along with the other body, since doing so would not cause the death of any person.

If, however, having a soul is what makes a human being biologically alive, then it seems odd that the thoracopagus or dicephalic (highly conjoined) twins should have two souls despite having only one set of vital organs (with the exception of the brain), while the cephalopagus twins should have two sets of vital organs (with the exception of the brain) and yet possess only one soul.

How does the naturalist account for these unusual cases? For the naturalist, what gives a human being special moral status is some psychological capacity or set of capacities, such as rationality, consciousness, self-awareness, capacity for human emotions, and so on. In other words, having a mind. Thoracopagus and dicephalic twins, as well as easily separable twins such as Chang and Eng, are two distinct persons because they have two distinct minds. (If I whisper something in Abby's ear, Brittany will not know what I said. Their thoughts are separate and independent of each other.) The cephalopagus twins, on the other hand, are only one person since they (or rather, he/she) can have only one mind, one set of thoughts.

For the naturalist, being a person is distinct from being alive. Being alive is, of course, a necessary condition for being a person (if we exclude intelligent machines or vampires or other compelling fictions). But there is no one-to-one correspondence between persons (or minds) and living human bodies.

One body with two heads (and thus two separate minds) can be two persons. Also, a living human body can have no mind (and thus not be a person), as is the case with someone who is brain-dead or with babies born without brains (known as *anencephalics*).

One problem remains, and that is the question of whether the conjoined twins constitute one living organism or two separate organisms. It seems that the thoracopagus and dicephalic twins constitute one living organism—one body, even if two people. And omphalopagus twins like Chang and Eng, since they can be so easily separated, should be considered as two living organisms that happen to be connected. But then what about conjoined twins that lie between these two extremes? More conjoined than Chang and Eng but less conjoined than Abby and Brittany? The naturalist might not be able to determine, in a nonarbitrary way, an exact point at which a pair of conjoined twins constitutes one biological organism or two distinct biological organisms. On the other hand, the naturalist can simply say that it does not matter whether we can say with certainty whether a pair of conjoined twins makes up one biological life or two biological lives because, on the naturalist view, being biologically alive is not what has moral significance. What is important is being a person, and conjoined twins do not present any difficulties there. With the exception of cephalopagus twins, who have only one brain, all conjoined twins consist of two persons because they have two distinct minds with their own separate thoughts.

ONE FROM TWO

Perhaps the most difficult case of abnormal human development for the vitalist to reconcile with his notion of life and the soul is the case of the genetic *chimera*. The chimera is in some sense the opposite of identical twins. Identical twins start out as one individual human embryo that later splits into two identical embryos, which develop into two different people with identical sets of genes. With the chimera, however, there is at first two distinct nonidentical (sometimes called "fraternal") twins originating from two different egg cells fertilized by two different sperm cells. Then, at some very early stage, these two distinct embryos fuse together and develop into one human being with two distinct sets of genes. The result is one person who is (usually) anatomically normal (no extra limbs or heads or anything) but has two sets of DNA in her body. Half of her cells have one set of genes—supplied by one of the original embryos—and the other half have a different set—supplied by the other original embryo. Sometimes a chimera might have two different blood types coursing through her veins. Or sometimes the two different sets of genes are coded for different skin colors and some of the person's skin will be darker and some lighter—typically with sharp borders indicting where the early embryos originally fused together.

These strange phenomena—two different skin tones, two different blood types, and so on—are indicators of this rare condition. Often, however, no such indicators are available because the cell specialization did not divide evenly across the two different sets of cells. When they first fuse, the cells have not yet specialized into nerve cells, skin cells, bone cells, and so on, but are still undifferentiated stem cells. What often happens with a chimera is that the cells from one embryo mostly specialize into the internal organs and the brain (for example), while the cells from the other embryo mostly specialize into skin and bone and muscle. Thus the two sets of genetic codes are not evenly dispersed throughout the body. Some parts have one genetic code and other parts have another genetic code.

How does vitalism map onto the phenomenon of chimerism? If life begins at conception, and life consists in having a soul, then each of the two original fertilized eggs had its own soul. But then the question is: Does the resulting individual have two souls? This does not seem likely since he or she is only one person with only one biological life. (A chimerical human can die only once, just like an ordinary human.) On the other hand, if the chimera has only one soul, then what happened to the two original souls? It does not seem reasonable to claim that one of the souls is no longer present in the individual. For one, that leads to the same problem of asymmetry that we saw in the identical twin case. Here the problem is the same, only in reverse. If the resultant person has only one of the original souls, then which one does the person have? It seems arbitrary to say one or the other since the individual body is composed of living cells that came from each of the original embryos. Besides the asymmetry problem, however, there is a further problem. If the resulting individual has only one soul, then what happened to the other soul? If one of the embryos lost its soul, then it must have died, since vitalism identifies the soul with life and the loss of soul with biological death. But it is clearly false to say that either of the original embryos died. Both of them continued to thrive and develop and grow—but into only one individual person (or, if you prefer, each into approximately one half of an individual person). Furthermore, if one embryo loses its soul, then the other embryo's soul must take over the new territory formerly inhabited by the departed soul. So, if life on the vitalist model is present from the moment of conception, and the chimera in the end has only one soul, then one of the souls, arbitrarily chosen, must leave. Yet the embryo does not die because there is a transfer of title over the material of the embryo from the departed soul over to the remaining soul. Although there might not be anything flatly contradictory in any of this, it does seem terribly clumsy.

There is another possibility. As the with the identical twin problem, which could be solved by allowing the soul to fission, we could solve the chimera problem by allowing the souls to fuse. I suspect, however, that soul fusion would be even less palatable to the vitalist than the soul fission.

Does the naturalist view of biological life map onto the strange case of the human chimera more effectively than vitalism? For naturalism, the embryo is a cluster of cells, living human cells that have the potential to develop into a human person like you or me. But there is no *further* entity that makes cells into a living thing. So when two cell clusters fuse together to form one cluster, the fully developed chimerical human person is one person. It does not matter that he has two distinct sets of genetic codes; he has one heart, one pair of lungs, one body, and, most important, one mind. It does not matter that he was once two discrete individuals; he is now one person with one whole body. His origin from two different embryos matters no more than the fact that all of us nonchimerical humans started off as one sperm and one egg cell that fused together. And if we must ask which of the two original embryos is identical to the fully developed chimera, we would say both of them (or each is identical to half of the person). It is no more of a problem than asking whether you originated from your father's sperm cell or from your mother's egg cell. You came from both.

THE HUMAN PARASITE

It is time now to consider the strangest and most disconcerting of the cases of abnormal human development—the parasitic twin. But before we do, we should briefly consider another unusual biological phenomenon called a *ter-atoma*. This is not a case of abnormal reproduction or development, but it has

its important similarities and differences to certain cases in human reproduction and so can help us to appreciate them. A teratoma is a tumor that
develops from germ cells in the ovaries or testicles. Some of these cells start
multiplying, eventually forming a tumor. These tumors can become quite
large. What makes a teratoma so unusual is that the cells of the tumor dif-
ferentiate into other kinds of specialized human cells. So the resulting tumor
can end up having lung tissue, fatty tissue, hair, teeth, and even nerve cells.
However, these various human parts that comprise the tumor are all jumbled
up. They are not organized into any coherent structures.

It seems that the teratoma offers no special problem for vitalism. The
tumor was not the product of conception and, since life begins at conception,
was never an individual living human being. Yes, the tumor is biologically
alive, but it is not a human being. It may be made of human cells and tissues—so it is alive and it is human—but it is not *a* human. It is merely a part
(although an abnormal, superfluous part) of the human being who has the
tumor. In this way it is no different from any other tumor or abnormal
growth. The fact that it has hair or teeth is not a problem. The teeth are not
the tumor's teeth, but rather the person with the tumor has extra teeth
growing in a strange place. So the teratoma is not a special problem for
vitalism or for naturalism. But it may help us to appreciate the troubling
nature of the parasitic twin.

One way in which twins can be born connected together is by being conjoined, which we discussed above. Conjoined twins are identical twins that
do not fully separate and often share certain body parts. Sometimes, however, when identical twins do not fully separate, the result is a pair of non-
symmetrical conjoined twins consisting of one fully developed person with
an underdeveloped twin—the parasitic twin—attached to his or her body.
This type of case starts with a single zygote (one egg fertilized by a single
sperm) that starts to develop into one embryo. At some point it divides, as in
identical twins, but the division is incomplete, so it starts to develop into conjoined twins. But then one of the twins stops developing or most of the twin
stops developing and parts of it continue to develop. What often results is a
fully developed human being with extra parts—the parts of the parasitic twin
that continued to develop. There might be an extra arm or an extra pair of
legs, though usually such limbs are severely atrophied. In most cases, this
parasitic twin has no brain or heart or any vital organs and lives off of the
blood supply of the fully developed person, or "host." But this is not always

the case. There have been a few instances of parasitic twin heads (known as *craniopagus parasiticus*).

Such cases of parasitic twins—asymmetrical conjoined twins—are interesting and raise problems for vitalism, but these problems are not that much different from the other problems raised by symmetrical conjoined twins. There is, however, a different kind of parasitic twin that raises a host of new questions and puzzles: the *fetus in fetu*. The rare fetus in fetu is a parasitic twin in the abdominal cavity of the host (the fully developed, otherwise normal twin). What makes the fetus in fetu so unusual, and different from a conjoined parasitic twin, is that it does not share any body parts in common with the host. It is embedded in the abdominal cavity of the host, but it is an entirely distinct and separate entity. It is contained in something like an amniotic sac or placenta with capillaries that absorb nutrients and oxygen from the host's blood. In this way the fetus in fetu is much like a pregnancy—it is almost as if the person with this condition was born pregnant with his or her own twin. It is, of course, very different from pregnancy in many obvious and important ways. For one, it is not a form of reproduction. The fetus in fetu is not the offspring of the host but the twin. Also, the fetus in fetu is not inside a uterus but simply in the no man's land of the abdominal cavity outside of the organs (stomach, liver, intestines, kidney, etc.). It is almost like an extra organ that was once a twin embryo.

Although the fetus in fetu is alive and may continue to live indefinitely inside its host, it grows only very slowly and will never develop into a normal human being. It is not preparing for anything like birth and would never be able to live removed from the host. Getting its nourishment and oxygen from the host's blood, it does not have lungs or a heart or a digestive tract. It is a parasite in the true sense of the word.

Although it lacks essential organs, the fetus in fetu is not just a mere clump of human cells like a tumor. It has skin on the outside and hair growing out of that skin. It has bones (though not a complete human skeleton), including a primitive backbone and long bones resembling undeveloped legs. It has a skull, or skull-like bone, with a large cavity, as if for a brain. The cavity is empty, however, containing only fluid instead of a brain. It also has no eyes, but it has indentations where eye sockets might have been, as well as wrinkles in the skin where facial features might have formed had it continued to develop. There is no mouth and no anus. It doesn't need either, since it feeds and breathes (gets its oxygen) from an umbilical cord attached to the sac that surrounds it, and collects nourishment and oxygen from the blood of the host.

There has been some debate among medical experts as to the exact nature and origin of the fetus in fetu. Some used to believe that it is merely a "highly organized teratoma." The more likely explanation, however, is that the fetus in fetu started out as a separate identical twin with its own amniotic sac but was within the same chorion (the membrane outside of the amnion that forms the inner layer of the placenta). For whatever reason, very early in the development, the twin fails to develop at the normal pace and the other twin continues to grow around it and eventually envelops it. This enveloped twin is kept alive by its umbilical cord, which is now connected to the inside of the normally developing twin who has grown around it. The fetus in fetu continues to grow slowly, but it does not develop. It does not develop organs or a brain—either because it does not get enough nutrients (since it is getting its nutrients from the leftovers of the twin fetus and not directly from the mother) or for the same reason that slowed its development in the first place. On the other hand, it does not need vital organs since even after birth (i.e., the birth of its host) it will still be inside someone else's body.

The challenge for the vitalist is to determine whether the fetus in fetu parasite has a soul. First, let us assume that the fetus in fetu results from a fully separated identical twin that fails to develop and is absorbed by the other twin. On the vitalist theory, the fetus in fetu would have a soul from the moment of conception (or at the moment of the fission that resulted in two identical twin embryos from one embryo). Since it did not die, nor did it form into an integrated part of the other, fully developed twin, then it must still have a soul. On the other hand, suppose that the rejected theory, that the fetus in fetu is merely a highly organized teratoma, were the correct one. Presumably the twin would not have a soul, since it never was conceived but just spontaneously started growing out of one of the host's cells. It would merely be a tumor and part of, although an unwanted part of, the body of the host—no matter how much it seemed to be distinct. This theory is not as unlikely as it may seem. Certain lizards, salamanders, and even turkeys are capable of reproducing this way. It is known as *parthenogenesis*. Basically what happens is one of the egg cells of the female simply starts to develop into an offspring instead of dividing, which results in the offspring getting the other half of its DNA from a male's sperm. Since this offspring will have the exact same DNA as the mother, it will be a perfect clone—it will be essentially both the daughter and the identical twin sister of the mother. It is conceivable (even if not in fact the case) that the teratoma is merely a botched parthenogenesis, and the fetus in fetu is merely a more successful attempt at asexual human reproduction.

Now, it seems that vitalism has a strange implication. If the fetus in fetu is a twin that was absorbed by its sibling in utero, then it has a soul; whereas if the fetus in fetu were a spontaneously developing tumor, it would not have a soul. It seems odd that whether or not this entity has a soul (or has "Life," in the substantive vitalist sense) depends solely on how it came to be and not what it is like now.

CLONING

The vitalist might protest that the fetus in fetu probably is not spontaneously generated but only results from one twin being enveloped by the other early in the development. But that does not matter. True, human beings are not capable of natural parthenogenesis, but they may one day be capable of a sort of *artificial* parthenogenesis by means of cloning. If Life, in the capital *L* vitalist sense, begins at conception, then at what moment begins the life of a person who was cloned from another person's cells? It is very likely that, given a few advancements in technology, one could take a sample of cells from my skin and make a clone of me. (This clone would essentially be my identical twin, but he would be much younger than me.) This clone could be implanted into a woman's uterus and would develop into a fully developed human baby and be born naturally. The resulting baby could then grow up and do all of the things that you and I can do; it would have all of the same kinds of thoughts and experiences we do. It seems absurd to say that this clone does not have a soul simply because it was not conceived in the usual way. (Any moral objections one might have to cloning are irrelevant. Even if it is wrong to do so, the fact that it is possible is a problem for vitalism. I myself have serious moral objections to cloning human beings, but not for any of the reasons discussed here.)

One might be tempted to say that this clone obtains its soul as soon as it starts to develop into a person—in other words, as soon as the scientist begins multiplying the skins cells he collected from me. But this leads to other problem for vitalism. A common treatment for severe burn victims is to harvest skin cells from uninjured parts of the victim's body and then multiply them in a petri dish. These cultivated skin cells are then reapplied in a very thin layer over the patient's burns, where it is hoped they will continue to multiply and eventually form new skin over the wounds. If a skin cell obtains a human soul as soon as it begins to divide in a petri dish, then these skin cultures would have a soul. Then the patient, once healed, would have the bizarre condition of having his regular soul, and part of his skin having its own soul.

One might object that the skin cells used for treating burns will never develop into a separate individual and so will never have a soul. But then it seems that the intentions of the scientist determine whether or not this multiplying cluster of cells has a soul. This does not work because the scientist's intentions could change. Suppose that a scientist is trying to make a clone of me from some skin cells that he collected, but shortly after he starts the procedure I suffer from third-degree burns. He then decides to change the nature of his project and continues to multiply these skins cells for the purpose of healing my burns. Did the cells have a soul when the scientist was making a clone but then cease to have a soul when he decided to use the cells to treat my burns?

NATURALISM AND THE PARASITIC TWIN

Let's turn our attention now to the naturalist's view of human life. On this view, the fetus in fetu—whether a spontaneously generated, highly organized teratoma or an identical twin enveloped by its sibling in the womb—is alive in the sense that it is composed of living human tissue. Is it a human being? Well, it has human DNA and is made of human tissues, but it does not have a human physiology. (Human beings, as a species, are not parasitic). The naturalist might not be able to answer this question with any precision, but it does not matter. As with the conjoined twins, the naturalist is not uncomfortable with biological entities that are only partly but not completely distinct. For vitalism, it must be an all-or-nothing affair; there must be either one complete human life or two distinct human lives. This is because, on this view, a human life is some further thing over and above the physiology and psychology. But for the naturalist, something can be one living human being in one sense but two living human beings in another. It can be two persons but only one living organism, as in the case of highly conjoined twins. Or it can be two distinct bodies but only one person, as with the fetus in fetu. Although it is inside the host and connected to the host through an umbilical cord, it is clearly a distinct living entity since the two do not share any parts in common. But there is only one person. The fetus in fetu is not, nor ever will be, a person since it has no brain and no capacity even for sensations, let alone human thoughts or feelings. For the naturalist, there is nothing morally wrong with removing the fetus in fetu from the host even though it will die shortly thereafter. For the substantive vitalist, who adheres to the sanctity of life, it would be morally wrong to remove the fetus in fetu because doing so would result in the death of a living human being—even though this human is not a person and has no potential for ever becoming one.

CONCLUSION TO PART ONE

What can we conclude from all of this? What we have seen is that the naturalist view of what constitutes human life maps onto what we know about the facts of human reproduction and development better than does substantive vitalism. This battle has taken place on a fair and neutral playing field because both sides presumably agree on the facts about human reproduction and development. Both agree that the (biological) life of an individual human being begins at conception when the man's sperm fertilizes the woman's egg cell, and that the resulting cell—with the complete and new set of DNA—divides and multiplies and eventually develops into a fetus. Both agree that identical twins result from a single embryo that divides very early in its development into two identical embryos, and that sometimes this division is incomplete, resulting in conjoined twins. The vitalists cannot say that this is an unfair forum for the debate unless they are prepared to dispute these facts. But they cannot reject the concept of conception if they want to maintain that life begins at conception. They cannot deny that identical twins do not exist, for we can easily show examples of them. And they can hardly deny that identical twins start out as a single embryo that divides into two because then they would have to come up with a new explanation of conjoined twins.

Instead of identifying what makes humans morally special with what makes us biologically alive, we would do better by identifying it with that which makes us persons: consciousness, the capacity for rational thought, or the ability to have human feelings, and so forth. We can adopt the naturalist perspective without denying that human beings, or at least most normal human beings, have a special moral status that elevates them above other animals. There is nothing supernatural about personhood. It consists of normal, observable psychological capacities.

So what are the implications for the abortion issue if we reject substantive vitalism? The most immediate implication is that one popular support for the antiabortion stance should be rejected. The sanctity of life principle, based on vitalism, has been shown to rely on a set of beliefs that do not fit with other things that we know about the world, and in particular about conception and early human development. Given that we are probably not willing to give up our biological knowledge (and all the useful medical treatments that that knowledge brings), we must give up vitalism and the sanctity of life principle that it supports. If the possession of a soul of the vitalist sort is not what makes a human being have moral worth, then what does? According to the naturalist, human beings have moral worth—and a moral worth greater than dogs and cats and sheep and other nonhuman animals—because of those qualities that make us a person. There may be some disagreement over exactly what these qualities are, but they will involve psychological states or capacities, such as the capacity for rational thought, human emotions, moral deliberation, or self-awareness. The strength of this view is that it does not matter, morally speaking, whether or not a human being has a soul. These properties, as well as the capacity to feel pleasure and pain, which even many nonhuman animals possess, is enough reason for us to think that anything that possesses these characteristics gives us moral duties toward it (for example, not to harm it or kill it unnecessarily). Thus we can determine what things have moral rights or deserve moral consideration without appealing to anything supernatural.

Although one support of the pro-life position is refuted, this is not the end of the debate. There are many arguments on both sides that do not rely on a particular worldview or a theory of what constitutes biological life. We need to consider these arguments next.

SUGGESTED FURTHER READING

Morowitz, Harold J., and James S. Trefil. *The Facts of Life: Science and the Abortion Controversy*. New York: Oxford University Press, 1992.

PART 2

The alleged existence of the soul is just one form of argument on the morality of abortion that is often given by nonphilosophers. There are other arguments that make no appeal to any supernatural objects or properties. Some of these arguments are given mostly by nonphilosophers, while some of them are taken seriously by philosophers as well.

In part 2 of this book we will consider three categories of arguments against abortion: responsibility, potentiality, and the golden rule. I say three "categories" rather than three arguments because there are many variations of each of these three argument types, some rather crude and some quite sophisticated. We will carefully consider these sorts of arguments in chapters 5, 6, and 7. In chapter 8 we will consider arguments based on the rights of the pregnant woman to terminate her pregnancy. In chapter 9 we will look at the consequences involved: both the consequences of having an abortion and the consequences of allowing or banning abortion. Both the pro-life and the pro-choice side appeal to consequences. Finally, in chapter 10, we will briefly examine how our attitudes about abortion reflect on our moral character.

CHAPTER 5

RESPONSIBILITY

THE RESPONSIBILITY ARGUMENT

In my several years of teaching philosophy—and in particular applied ethics—I have encountered many versions of what I will call the "responsibility" argument in student papers arguing for the pro-life position. Whether these are merely different versions of the same argument or distinctly different arguments is not really important. I cluster them together only because they seem to be motivated by the same sorts of attitudes and center around that one word *responsible* (or variations of that root word, including *irresponsible*, *responsibility*, etc.). I am careful to say that these various arguments center around a particular *word*, not on the same concept, because "responsibility" has many different, though closely related, meanings; and it is not clear that all of my students are using the word in the same sense. Different students seem to be appealing to different concepts of "responsibility" and thus seem to be presenting slightly different arguments.

One feature that most of these arguments have in common is that, unlike the other arguments we will consider, they are generally weak and ill formulated and are therefore easy to refute. That being said, it is important that we do not assume, just because *these* pro-life arguments are weak, that the entire pro-life position is weak. A bad argument can still have a true conclusion. Consider this argument:

(1) All edible animals can fly.
(2) Pigs can fly.
(3) Therefore, pigs are edible animals.

This is a very weak argument. Not only are the two premises (1) and (2) false, but even if they were true, the conclusion would not necessarily follow. Thus the argument must be rejected. But that does not mean we should reject the conclusion of the argument. In fact, the conclusion is obviously true. If we did not already know that pigs are edible, however, then we would have to suspend judgment—we could not accept it as true, but we also could not reject it as false. If we had to judge on the basis of this bad argument alone, we would have to admit that it could be as likely true as false.

Thus I present these weak versions of the responsibility argument on the pro-life side not as an attempt to discredit the antiabortion position, but so that we can see why these arguments are weak and thus get rid of them. We need to do this because they are, judging from my students' papers, fairly popular. Bad arguments that have some popularity are like counterfeit currency. In much the same way that counterfeit currency is falsely taken to have purchasing power, these weak arguments are falsely taken to support their conclusion. We thus need to take them out of circulation.

PUNISHMENT FOR THEIR SINS

One of the weakest arguments that I find in some student papers goes something like this. Having to bear the fetus and give birth to it is a fitting punishment for some wrongdoing (presumably unprotected sex) on the part of the pregnant woman. (People who offer this version of the responsibility argument almost invariably approve of abortion in the case of rape.) Of course, rarely is the argument laid out in so stark a fashion. More often it is only made implicitly. The students will hint at this sort of rationalization of their pro-life stance through vague clichés such as "she made her bed and now she should have to lie in it," or "you play, you pay," or—less poetically—"that's what she gets."

Where does such a lame argument come from? My guess is that it is part of the rhetoric that pervades public discourse. Some people who would never consider abortion an option for themselves sympathize with women whose lives are adversely affected—possibly ruined—by an unwanted pregnancy. Because of their feelings of sympathy, these people see abortion in a more favorable light. To combat this, the pro-life side tries to vilify the women who wish to get an abortion. If they can cast the women in a negative light, then people will be less inclined to sympathize with them or their reasons for wanting an abortion. Another possible explanation is what social psychologists call the just world hypothesis. We humans have a natural tendency to assume that victims of misfortune somehow deserve it. It allows us to maintain the comforting thought that life is, for the most part, fair. Of course, none of this has anything to do with whether or not abortion is morally permissible. Just because we tend to sympathize with someone does not make his or her action morally right, and just because we fail to sympathize with someone does not make his or her action wrong. The problem is that some students take a rhetorical device meant to emotionally manipulate people into changing their attitudes and try to use it as an argument.

There are several problems with this "argument." The first is that in order to deserve punishment one must have done something wrong. I suspect that many students who use this version of the responsibility argument see sex itself as dirty and sinful and think that the woman is doing wrong by engaging in sex. This is not at all plausible. Sex is a normal, natural, healthy human activity. As long as both parties are freely consenting adults, there shouldn't be any moral objection. There are some sexual acts that some might consider to be objectionable, such as prostitution or adultery. But it is not clear that prostitutes are genuinely free from coercion. And with adultery, it is not the sex per se that is morally wrong but the breaking of vows and the betrayal of trust. If, however, no one is harmed, no one is being coerced or having his or her rights violated, and no one is being treated unfairly, then I cannot see how having sex could be thought of as morally wrong. Certainly (unforced) sex between married couples is not morally wrong, but I doubt that these students would be any more approving of married women having abortions than single women.

What about getting pregnant? Surely there is nothing wrong with getting pregnant, as long as the mother is not endangering her own life to do so. A woman who wants to have children, who can easily afford it, and who would be a good parent is not doing anything morally wrong by getting pregnant. One might argue that given the overpopulation of the earth, it is morally wrong to have children. But clearly this could not be used as part of an argument to support the pro-life position. The overpopulation problem would be a point in favor of abortion, since having an abortion would help to slow the population growth.

If neither having sex nor getting pregnant is morally wrong, per se, then what is the punishment for? One might suggest that having an *unwanted* pregnancy is morally wrong. But that is a very strange claim, for if there is nothing wrong with becoming pregnant, then the only thing that could be wrong with an unwanted pregnancy would be the unwanted aspect of it. But I do not see how someone could deserve punishment for not wanting something. People deserve punishment for what they do, not for what they want or do not want, and not for being displeased with what happens to them.

One might be tempted to say that what is morally objectionable about an unwanted pregnancy is the carelessness of the woman in getting pregnant. And indeed, this is what some of the less reflective students seem to say. (They never consider the carelessness of the man, but let's set that aside.) Sometimes carelessness does deserve blame and punishment. We rightly disapprove of parents who allow their toddlers to wander unattended; and we rightly punish drunk or reckless drivers. But carelessness is morally objectionable only when it leads to, or is likely to lead to, some harm to others. It is the potential harmful result of the carelessness that constitutes the wrongdoing in the case of the negligent parent or the reckless driver, not the carelessness itself. No one would condemn a woman who became pregnant through carelessness but then welcomed the surprise, had the child, and was a loving and nurturing mother. Thus, the only difference is the fact that the pregnancy is unwanted.

Carelessly getting pregnant could be morally objectionable only if there were some harm or wrongdoing resulting from, or likely to result from, the carelessness. Could one argue that carelessly getting pregnant is wrong because it is likely to lead to an abortion? The problem with this is that it already assumes that an abortion is morally wrong, and that is the issue we are debating. If you are giving an argument that abortion is wrong, you cannot already assume that abortion is wrong as part of your argument. That would be what philosophers call *begging the question*. (More on this later.)

Perhaps we could argue that having an abortion constitutes some kind of harm, and so carelessly getting pregnant is wrong because it is likely to lead to some harm. We will consider in the next chapter how an abortion might be thought of as harming a person. But the issue is irrelevant here. Even if abortion harms some person, that could only make the *abortion* wrong, not the carelessly getting pregnant. The problem with this fitting-punishment version of the responsibility argument is that if the harm is the abortion, then that does not explain how being forced to carry the fetus full term and giving birth can be a deserved punishment. Prior to the abortion there has not been any harm, and if the woman is prevented from having the abortion, then it is not clear what harm or wrongdoing the woman committed in becoming pregnant. If she did nothing wrong in carelessly becoming pregnant, then it is not clear what she deserves to be punished for. If having to carry the fetus and give birth is to be some kind of punishment, then there must be some kind of wrongful act committed even when the woman does not have the abortion.

Of course, there is something even more objectionable to the fitting-punishment version of the responsibility argument against abortion. Making someone carry a fetus full term and give birth to it would be a barbaric (not to mention bizarre) form of punishment. Could you imagine a society that punished criminals that way? Suppose a man is convicted of a serious crime, such as armed robbery, and we implant an embryo inside of him and force him to give birth to it. (I suppose we would have to do a cesarean.) It would take a sick mind to even contemplate this form of punishment. Even more repulsive is the attitude toward children that this kind of argument indicates— that they should be used as tools for punishing people. I certainly hope no one thinks this way on careful reflection. And if some people do think this way, I hope they never have children of their own. But perhaps those who make this sort of argument are thinking of "fitting punishment" in the sense of cosmic justice, or karma, or punishment by God—not as something that we ourselves would ever impose on someone.

GETTING AN ABORTION IS IRRESPONSIBLE

The number of students who have implied that pregnancy and childbirth should be thought of as some kind of punishment is, fortunately, pretty small. More often, students who give some version of the responsibility argument express a more reasonable motivation for their antiabortion stance. This argument generally focuses on the negative term *irresponsible* and applies this term to the woman who has an abortion or to the act of having an abortion. These students, in one way or another, denounce either the abortion as being an irresponsible act or those who have abortions as being irresponsible people for doing so. Sometimes they formulate their position in more positive terms by praising the act of carrying an unwanted fetus full term and giving birth to it as the "responsible thing to do." This version of the responsibility argument is better than the fitting-punishment version because it is the abortion itself, and/or those who actually have an abortion, that is condemned as being irresponsible—not those who, for whatever reason, find themselves with an unwanted pregnancy.

The frequency with which students present this kind of argument indicates that it must have considerable intuitive appeal, or at least that it carries considerable rhetorical sway. There is, however, one major weakness with virtually every student paper I have read that gives this kind of antiabortion argument: not one of them has ever tried to explain exactly—or even roughly—what "irresponsible" means (or what any of its cognates such "responsible," "responsibility," etc., mean). Without explaining exactly what it means to be "irresponsible" or to act "irresponsibly," we cannot assess the claim that abortion is irresponsible—let alone determine whether it is a reason for being opposed to abortion. Without a clear definition of "irresponsible," the accusation that abortion is irresponsible is just pure rhetoric. When we hear the word "irresponsible," we know that it is term of condemnation, and it makes us inclined to oppose whatever it is applied to. But without a definition we are in no position to judge whether abortion is irresponsible.

IRRESPONSIBLE AS EQUIVALENT TO MORALLY WRONG

One meaning of the term "irresponsible" is roughly equivalent to "careless." But, as we saw earlier, to act in a careless manner is not necessarily to do anything morally wrong and is not by itself any reason to oppose such acts. If I dress myself carelessly, I might miss a button or put on socks that don't match, but I am not thereby doing anything morally objectionable. This is not just a matter of degree. I could dress myself *very* carelessly, even *recklessly*—perhaps my underwear would end up on the outside. But that still does not seem to be a moral issue. Carelessness is morally objectionable when it is likely to lead to harm, and then it is morally objectionable for the harm that it is likely to cause, not for the sloppy manner in which the act was done. But *irresponsible* doesn't just mean the same as *careless*, for no matter how sloppily I dress myself, no one would say that I dressed irresponsibly.

It is clear from reading their papers that some of my students who present the responsibility argument use the term *irresponsible* to mean roughly "morally wrong." The problem with this argument is that it is obviously question begging. To *beg the question* in the sense that philosophers and logicians use the phrase is to already assume in your argument the truth of the conclusion you are arguing for. *Question* here basically means "the issue under debate," and *to beg* means roughly "to pull a fast one." (This is, of course, not a literal translation.) To beg the question is to commit a *fallacy*, some sort of mistake in reasoning, intentionally or accidentally, which is likely to mislead the careless or sympathetic listener. To say that a fallacy is a mistake is being somewhat charitable. Often people commit fallacies on purpose because they do not have a good argument, and so they resort to deceptive arguments, or pseudoarguments, to trick people into believing what they want them to believe. The important thing is to understand that whenever you commit a fallacy you end up with a very weak argument or no argument, which gives you no reason to believe the conclusion.

The fallacy of begging the question works by slipping the conclusion (what is being argued for) into the premises (the evidence for the conclusion). In other words, it involves assuming to be true the very thing that you are trying to prove. Begging the question is to logic what using a term in its own definition is to lexicography. If you use a word (or variation of that word) in its own definition, then you are presenting a circular definition, which will not give the word's meaning. For example, if I define *excellence* as "the state or property of being excellent," then I have not defined it. Someone who did not know what *excellence* means would not be helped by this definition. Likewise, including the conclusion as part of the argument for the conclusion gets you nowhere. It will not persuade anyone who is not already convinced; and it gives no reason to think the conclusion is true (even if it is).

If *irresponsible* means roughly the same as *morally wrong*, then it should be obvious how the responsibility argument goes afoul. The argument is roughly as follows:

Premise: Having an abortion is irresponsible.
Conclusion: Therefore, having an abortion is morally wrong.

But if *irresponsible* mean the same as *morally wrong*, then the premise means the same as the conclusion. We could substitute "morally wrong" for "irresponsible" in the premise, and then the argument would read like this:

Premise: Having an abortion is morally wrong.
Conclusion: Therefore, having an abortion is morally wrong.

We are merely assuming that the conclusion is true (that abortion is morally wrong) instead of inferring a conclusion from some evidence. We simply restate what has already been presumed to be true. Unless I am already convinced that abortion is wrong, then I would not accept the premise (specifically, that abortion is "irresponsible" in this sense). And of course, if I did accept the premise, then I would not need to draw a conclusion by way of a pseudoargument.

"How could anyone fall for such a simplistic argument?" you may ask. Let us not be too hasty in our condemnation. Many people do not understand what an argument is, or they confuse argument with debate and rhetoric. This is hardly surprising, given that political speeches and public debate rarely rise above the level of a sales pitch and often sink to the level of mindless slogans and vicious name-calling. I think that after careful reflection many people who would debate along these lines would concede that they were not making an actual argument—at least not in the sense that we usually define an argument. Instead they were simply explaining their position. They think that abortion is irresponsible, or *in other words*, morally wrong. These two claims need not be linked as premise and conclusion but could be merely two different ways of stating the same thing. If that is the case, then no fallacy is committed. But if that is the case, then we are presented with no reason to disapprove of abortion if we do not already do so.

ACCEPTING RESPONSIBILITY

Let us switch from the negative term *irresponsible* to its positive root term, *responsible*, in order to analyze a different concept. Another version of the responsibility argument starts with the claim that the pregnant woman is responsible for the fetus. What does this mean?

One definition of the term *responsible* means simply "to be the cause of something." Back in college I had a '63 Nova. One day, it suddenly stopped running, so I had my mechanic friend take a look. We discovered that the wiring was completely burnt out and that a wire had shaken loose from the alternator and grounded, causing a short. We also noticed that the bracket holding the alternator in place was broken. Having discovered all this, I might have said something like "The broken alternator bracket was *responsible* for the eventual engine failure." Certainly this sense of *responsible* has no moral sense. The alternator bracket was not evil for sabotaging my car. (It is worth noting that *responsible* in this sense has no complimentary sense of *irresponsible*. I might say that the battery was "not responsible" for the engine failure, but it would make no sense to say that the battery was "irresponsible" for the engine failure!)

There is, however, another sense of *responsible* that might have some moral connotation. This sense of *responsible* means "to be accountable" for one's actions. To be accountable means accepting the blame or facing the deserved consequences of one's own actions or choices. (And the corresponding sense of *irresponsible* means ducking the blame or avoiding the consequences.) We especially mean this when we say that someone *takes* responsibility for his actions. Let us examine the possible interpretations of this sense of being responsible and see (1) whether having an abortion is irresponsible in this sense and, if so, (2) whether this provides us with any reason for thinking that abortion is wrong.

Let's start with the first interpretation of responsibility-as-accountability: accepting blame and/or punishment. If I smash into a parked car late at night and no one is around to witness it, I may be able to sneak away without getting caught and thus not have to compensate the owner. In this situation we would say that the "responsible thing to do" would be for me to leave a note on the windshield with information as to where I can be contacted, or to come back later and try to find the owner. By acting thusly, I am accepting blame and making amends—taking responsibility for my actions.

The problem with this interpretation of *responsibility* is that it does not work as an argument for why abortion is wrong. To be willing to accept blame or punishment, in the usual sense, I must believe myself to have done something wrong or to have harmed some innocent person (i.e., I must have done something worthy of blame or punishment, or at least requiring reparations). But simply by getting pregnant, a woman has not necessarily done anything wrong or harmful. If we use *responsibility* in this sense, then the responsibility argument ends up being similar to the fitting-punishment argument that we have already rejected. Furthermore, even if there were something morally objectionable about getting pregnant, it is not at all clear how carrying the fetus full term and giving birth to it (against one's own preferences) would in any way be making amends for that wrongdoing. Even if we think the woman "owes it" to the fetus to deliver it into the world (as the pro-lifers believe) she would not owe it because of any wrong or harm that she has done to the fetus (unlike the case in which I crash into someone's parked car).

One might argue that it was a *mistake* to get pregnant, insofar as it is an unwanted pregnancy. But we must be careful to distinguish personal mistakes from moral errors. A moral mistake is one for which we must apologize or make amends, and for which we might even deserve punishment. In the example of crashing into the parked car, presumably I did not do it on purpose, but it was a mistake. Nevertheless, it is a moral issue because I have harmed someone and so owe her some apology and compensation. But some mistakes do not require any apology or justification. If I make an egregious error on a crossword puzzle, I do not need to apologize to anyone for it. Even if it is a nontrivial mistake with serious consequences, as long as no one else is harmed I do not owe anything to anyone else, nor do I need to accept any blame. If, for example, I mistakenly put my car into first gear instead of reverse and crash it into my own house, I do not need to apologize to anyone or make amends (unless I shared the house with family or friends). There is no blame for me to accept, and I do not need to inform others of what an idiot I was. So even if we accept that an unwanted pregnancy is a mistake, that does not necessarily mean that there was any wrongdoing or that there is any blame to be accepted.

What we are concerned with here is the argument that not aborting the fetus is the responsible thing to do—and on this interpretation *responsible* means accepting blame and/or making amends. If not having the abortion (carrying the fetus full term and birthing it) involves accepting some sort of blame, then the harm or wrongdoing must have *already occurred* before considering whether to have an abortion. It is nonsense to say that carrying the fetus full term is some way of making amends for the wrongdoing of aborting it. Clearly, not running into the parked car cannot be making amends for running into the parked car. If abortion is wrong, it cannot be because one has already committed a wrong and needs to make amends by having a baby. Giving birth cannot be the responsible thing to do in this sense of *responsible*.

FACING UP TO THE CONSEQUENCES

The other interpretation of responsibility-as-accountability involves facing up to the consequences of one's actions, especially when those are negative consequences to oneself. These can be the natural consequences of one's actions, as opposed to social consequences such as blame or punishment, and so they do not require any kind of wrongdoing or harm. Suppose, for example, that a student of mine fails to write a paper because he was out partying (not that any of my students would do such a thing!). The responsible thing for that student to do, in this sense of facing up to the consequences, would be to come to me, admit that he did not do the paper because he was partying, and "face the music," as they say. He would not be a responsible person if he tried to avoid the consequences of his laziness by cooking up some cock-and-bull story about how sick he has been lately. (Note that this might not be a lie; it might be true that he has been sick lately, especially if he has been doing a lot of partying.) It would also show a lack of responsibility if he tried to weasel out of getting a bad grade in some other way, such as having his rich and important father influence my grading. He did not do anything morally wrong by partying; he had no moral duty to write the paper. So this sense of *responsible* has nothing to do with blame or punishment. Being irresponsible in this sense is not a failure to accept blame or make amends but merely a failure to be accountable to the negative consequences of one's own imprudent behavior.

This is certainly an important aspect of what we mean by *responsibility*, and it is morally relevant. We have reason, I think, to disapprove of the student who is irresponsible in this way and to praise the student who is responsible in this way. There is something morally repugnant about the person who tries to weasel out of the consequences of his behavior and something admirable about one's willingness to own up to the consequences of what one does.

There seem to be two problems with applying this sense of being responsible (or irresponsible) to the woman who is considering having an abortion. For one, I tend to think of the student's partying as irresponsible—not in the sense of being morally wrong but merely imprudent or foolish, or in some similar way objectionable. For example, if the student failed to write the paper because he spent the weekend working for the Red Cross helping with disaster relief after a recent hurricane, and then tried to play on my sympathies with the storm victims in order to convince me to let him turn in the paper late, I would not be inclined to call that irresponsible.

The second, and more important, problem with applying this sense of *irresponsible* to the woman who is considering aborting her fetus is that it is not clear that she is trying to duck any negative consequences to herself. It is not as if she is trying to pretend that she is not pregnant; she is not trying to avoid her problem. Having an abortion is surely not a pleasant experience and is not something that one would normally choose to undergo or take lightly. It might be said that the abortion is one of the negative consequences of having an unwanted pregnancy. On this view, seeking out an abortion *is* facing up to the negative consequences of one's actions—just as is the case of the student who comes to me without excuses to face whatever hardship I will impose for his having not done the assignment. There are two ways of facing up to one's consequences: actively and passively. The student who comes to me without excuses to accept his poor grade is actively facing up to the consequences, while the student who sits at home waiting for his failing grade—expecting it and not complaining—does so passively. Similarly, the woman who gets an abortion when she finds out that she is pregnant is facing up to the consequences in an active sense. Surely one could make the case that having an abortion is more "responsible" than having more children when one does not have the means to raise them decently. This woman is acting more responsibly than the young woman who has the child and then leaves it with her elderly parents to raise while she goes out and parties with her friends.

The pro-lifer would no doubt accuse me of a false dichotomy. I have artificially limited the alternatives to having an abortion or raising the child oneself. There are clearly other alternatives, such as birthing the baby and then giving it up for adoption. But this misses the point. I am not arguing that there are only two alternatives—abortion and being a neglectful mother—and that, between the two, abortion is preferable. This claim would be very dubious even if these were the only two alternatives (unless the child were so badly abused and with no hope of salvation that it would be better off having never been born). I am simply comparing two of several alternatives and insisting that abortion is the more responsible of the two in the sense of *responsible* that we are considering here. This sense of *responsible* does not mean strictly "morally right" but simply means that one faces up to the negative consequences of one's actions. There are other responsible alternatives, such as birthing the baby and raising it in a loving, nurturing environment, or, if the woman knows herself to be incapable of decent parenting, birthing the baby and giving it up for adoption. We cannot just assume that one of these is morally preferable to the others, for the question under consideration is whether there is anything morally wrong with having an abortion. There needs to be some argument for the claim that abortion is wrong. The argument we are considering is that it involves failure to be accountable to the negative consequences of one's actions. And that is not obviously the case here.

RESPONSIBILITY FOR SOMEONE (OR SOMETHING)

There is one more sense of the word *responsible* that people think of when they describe having an abortion as being irresponsible. This is the sense in which we say that you are "responsible *for* someone or something." To say that something or someone is your responsibility is roughly to say that it is your job to take care of that something or someone. When a child gets a new puppy, for example, the parents might tell the child that the dog will be her responsibility. That means that it is her duty to make sure that the dog is taken care of. A dog needs to be watered, fed, walked, played with, disciplined, and loved. Someone has to do these things for the dog. To say that the dog is the child's responsibility is to say that *she* is that person who must do those things.

The version of the responsibility argument that is based on this sense of *responsible* starts with the assumption that the woman is responsible for the fetus. Of course she is usually (at least partly) responsible in the purely causal sense we discussed above—but this sense of responsibility is, by itself, not morally relevant. To be the cause of something does not mean that it is morally wrong to get rid of it. I am the cause of my own cigarette addiction, but that does not mean that I should keep smoking. I have no obligation to preserve my addiction. The claim being made in this sense of the responsibility argument is that the pregnant woman has a duty to take care of her fetus.

Before we can assess this argument we must determine exactly what we mean by "taking care of" someone or something. The most obvious sense of taking care of something means to protect it, provide for it, and nurture it.

This is the sense we mean when we say the child has a duty to take care of her new puppy. But another sense of *take care* of means roughly "to eliminate," as when a mob boss asks his trusted hit man to take care of a certain stoolie. When a mother tells her child to "take care of this mess," she certainly does not mean that the child should provide for the mess and nurture it. She means "get rid of it." It might seem obvious that this is not the sense of *taking care of* something that we mean when we say we have a "responsibility" for something. But let's not be too hasty. Often this is exactly what we mean we say that you are responsible for something or someone. For example, if a football coach says to one of his offensive linemen, "This man is your responsibility" (pointing to an X representing an opposing linebacker), what he means is that it is that lineman's job to take that opponent out of the play and eliminate him. He definitely does not mean that the lineman should protect and provide for the well-being of the opposing linebacker.

Maybe the unwanted fetus is the pregnant woman's responsibility in the sense that it is a mess that needs to be cleaned up by her—she needs to "take care of it" in the sense of getting rid of it, of dealing with the problem and solving it. Pro-lifers will, of course, sharply disagree, but they need some argument that explains why the fetus is her responsibility in the nurturing-and-providing sense and not in the cleaning-up-and-getting-rid-of sense. If the fetus is the woman's responsibility in the latter sense, then having an abortion would actually be the responsible thing to do, in the same way that cleaning up a mess that I caused would be the responsible thing to do rather than leaving it for someone else to clean up.

This might seem like just playing games with words. But this is why we need to get clear on the meaning of *responsibility*. The pro-life argument might rely on people agreeing that the fetus is the woman's responsibility in one sense (she caused it or she needs to do something about it) that most everyone will agree with, and then concludes that she is responsible for it in the sense that she must nurture it. This is a fallacy (i.e., mistake in reasoning) that philosophers refer to as *equivocation*. (See chapter 3.) An equivocation occurs when a term is used one way in part of the argument but then used a different way in another part of the argument. Consider the following:

(1) A Greyhound is a good source of transportation.
(2) My pet Fido is a greyhound.
(3) Therefore, my pet Fido is a good source of transportation.

This argument does not work because in premise (1) "Greyhound" refers to a commercial bus line, whereas in premise (2) "greyhound" refers to a breed of dog used for racing. Of course, the conclusion (3) would follow if we used the same term throughout the argument, but then one of the premises would obviously be false. Perhaps something similar is going on in the pro-life responsibility argument. It may be that there is confusion between these two senses of responsibility.

(1) The pregnant woman needs to do something about the fetus (i.e., is responsible for it in one sense).
(2) Therefore, she needs to nurture it (i.e., is responsible for it in a different sense).

The pro-choicer could agree with (1) but disagree with (2).

Let us just assume that having a "responsibility" for the unwanted fetus means having a duty to "take care of it" in the sense of nurturing it and providing for it. Given this interpretation, *if* the pregnant woman is responsible for her fetus, then it does seem to indicate that abortion would be morally wrong. Certainly getting rid of something is incompatible with caring for it and nurturing it. But now the argument suffers from the obvious flaw that most of the other versions of the responsibility argument suffer from: it begs the question. This argument starts with the claim that the pregnant woman has a duty to nurture the fetus, and thus a duty not to abort the fetus. But that is the very thing that the argument was intended to prove. We need some argument for why the pregnant woman should have responsibility for her fetus in this way.

Let us go back to the example of the dog. The child who demanded that her parents get a puppy has the responsibility for the dog. This obviously means that she is obligated to feed it, water it, walk it, and love it. Why is it obvious that this is the sense of responsibility intended? Because the dog is a pet, and pets are animals that we care for. The child has assumed this responsibility because she has brought the dog home from the pet store. And now that the dog is in her home, it will suffer without the child's care. (Had the child left the dog at the pet store, the dog would not require the child's care, although of course it would require care from someone.)

All of us (pro-lifers, pro-choicers, and those who are uncertain) might agree that the fetus is the pregnant woman's responsibility if we leave open what sort of responsibility this is—the responsibility to get rid of it and "clean it up" or the responsibility to care for it and nurture it. Which way her responsibility goes, and whether or not it is her choice, is what is under debate, and so we cannot start any argument that just assumes it to be one way or the other.

Note that it does no good to say, "It is her responsibility to nurture it *because she caused it to be* by choosing to have sex." This assumes that she has taken on that kind of responsibility by getting pregnant, just as the child has taken on that same kind of responsibility in bringing the puppy home. We could give the same reason for someone taking on the other kind of responsibility. "It is her responsibility to get rid of it [the fetus] *because she caused it to be*." In the same way we could say that the child is responsible for the dog crap on the floor because she caused it to be there by forgetting to take Fido for a walk.

The child's responsibility for the dog is to nurture it, not get rid of it. So we must ask whether the fetus is like the pet dog in a way that would make us think that the pregnant woman's responsibility to the fetus is to nurture it and not just "clean it up." It seems to me that the reason why the child has a duty to nurture the pup is (at least in part) that if the dog is not fed and watered and loved, then it will suffer. It would be wrong to neglect the dog (or eliminate the dog) because this will cause it pain. But the fetus, at least in the early stages when most abortions occur, is not capable of feeling pain, neither physical nor emotional. This is because the brain of the fetus is not sufficiently developed to have any perceptual capacity until at least the second trimester. (We will consider the issue of fetal pain again in chapter 9.) So there is a need for someone to take care of the dog, and since the family has taken it into their home, they have made it their duty to raise it properly. The substance of the duty—in other words, *what* it is a duty to do—has nothing to do with bringing it home. Rather the substance of the duty (to care for and nurture the pup) comes from the nature of the dog—its need for food, water, and love, as well as its capacity to feel physical and emotional suffering. Taking it into their home determines only whose duty it is, that is, who is the person that has this duty to raise the dog. Similarly, getting pregnant, if done on purpose (or at least not against her will), might make the fetus the woman's responsibility, but it does not determine the *substance* of what that responsibility is or *what* she is obligated to do about it. The substance of her duty might be to nurture it or to eliminate it (or to choose one or the other), and we cannot determine this merely by looking at the relationship between the pregnant woman and the fetus. The nature of her duty will depend at least in part on the nature of the fetus itself.

We already considered one argument based on the nature of the fetus in part 1. It is that the fetus has a substantive soul that makes it alive and that gives it a special moral status. We saw how that argument runs up against the facts of biology. Now let us consider, in the next two chapters, several more arguments against abortion that appeal to the nature of the fetus. We will first consider the argument based on the fetus's potential (its potential to be a person and its potential future life experiences) and then on the golden rule argument against abortion. Both of these arguments are based on the fact that the fetus will, under proper circumstances, develop into a full person just like you and me, and that each of us were, in fact, at one time a fetus before developing into the persons that we are now.

CHAPTER 6
THE POTENTIALITY ARGUMENT

I n chapters 2 through 4 we considered arguments against abortion based on the claim that the fetus possesses a substantive soul or a human "Life," with a capital *L*, that is, something over and above the mere biological processes, such as nutrition and growth. We found this approach to be wanting because of the difficulty reconciling this notion of a substantive soul (present from the point of conception) with what we know about how babies are made—in particular with the phenomena of twins and chimeras. Then, in chapter 5, we looked at arguments against abortion based on the *responsibilities* of the pregnant woman or the *irresponsibility* of having an abortion. These arguments were not so effective and suffered either from a vague concept of *responsibility* or from begging the question.

There are, however, other arguments in support of the claim that the fetus has a special moral status that do not appeal to any supernatural entity or property, and do not suffer the weaknesses of the responsibility arguments. One of these arguments—or more accurately, one class of such arguments— is based on the potential of the fetus. Arguments based on the potential of the fetus are not based on any properties that the fetus possesses now, at the time it is to be aborted, but instead they are based on properties that the fetus will have at some point in the future. On this view, it is not what the fetus is but what it will be that gives it special moral status. The argument is roughly that the fetus has a moral status identical (or at least similar) to persons because, although it is not a person now, it has the potential to become a person it the future.

POTENTIAL GREATNESS

One particularly crude version of the argument from potentiality is the old rhetorical challenge "What if the fetus to be aborted would have been the next Mozart?" There are as many particular versions of this as there are talented and renowned people. "What if it grew up to be the next Einstein?" ". . . Mother Teresa?" Or "What if this fetus grew up to cure cancer?" or ". . . solve world hunger?"

The argument seems to be that if the fetus were to eventually develop into a great person—someone who does great things of enormous benefit to humanity—then it would be wrong to kill the fetus and deny the world the benefits of this future greatness. This is a version of the potentiality argument, of course, because the fetus is not yet a great person—or even a person at all—and has not yet done anything, let alone anything of any merit or benefit to others.

It seems reasonable to have moral objections to aborting a fetus that might go on to achieve great success in art or science, or that will make some significant contribution to the well-being of a large number of people. Still, it is not clear exactly why. There are two possible supports for this claim. One version of this claim is supported by a *utilitarian* argument. The utilitarian theory claims that the rightness or wrongness of an action is determined entirely by the overall consequences of that act. Good consequences include increases in human happiness and decreases in human suffering, while bad consequences are decreases in happiness and increases in suffering. On this view, the right act would be whichever one would lead to the greatest overall increase (or least overall decrease) in the happiness of everyone affected. (We will look more closely at utilitarianism in chapter 9.)

Aborting the fetus might lead to somewhat more happiness for the pregnant woman who is not yet ready to bear a child. But if the fetus would have grown up to discover a cure for cancer, then denying the woman an abortion would ultimately lead to the prevention of a great amount of suffering, which would far outweigh the suffering of the woman who is forced to carry her pregnancy full term and give birth to the fetus against her will. (Of course, this assumes that someone else would not have cured cancer anyway.)

The other version of this "potential greatness" argument is not based on good consequences to others brought about by the future great person but on the claim that the existence of such a great person is itself of significant value, independent of the happiness she might cause or the pain she might prevent. This argument seems to imply that only the lives of great people have significant intrinsic value, or, at any rate, that the lives of such people are worth much more than the lives of ordinary people like you or me. But why must the fetus be a potential Mozart, Einstein, or Rembrandt for it to be wrong to terminate it? For whatever exact reason, this version of the potentiality argument against abortion claims that the lives of such great people is of so much value—either in itself or because of the good that would be brought to others—that it would be wrong to have an abortion because one would be preventing this great good.

The obvious problem with this argument is that, while it may be true that the fetus could grow up to be a great person like Einstein or Martin Luther King Jr., it could also grow up to be a terrible person like Hitler or Ted Bundy. As much good as we should ascribe to the fetus becoming a hero or a saint (either because of the inherent good of this person's life or because of the good consequences such a person would bring to others), we must ascribe to it an equivalent amount of badness should it grow up to be a monster or a villain (either for the inherent badness of this person's life or for the harm such a life would cause to others). And it seems just as likely that this fetus would grow up to be a bad person who causes suffering as it would be a good person who benefits others.

In fact, there is good reason to think that the fetus facing possible abortion would much more likely become a villain than a saint. Recently, economist Steven Levitt drew a rather controversial link between the reduction of crime starting in the 1990s and the legalizing of abortion in the early 1970s. The cause of the significant decline in the crime rate, according to Levitt, was the increased rate of abortions starting in 1973 when abortion was first legalized. The explanation behind this causal connection is that the majority of fetuses who were aborted would have been much more likely than the rest of the population to become criminals. This makes sense, given that most abortions are sought by young, single women with relatively little education and low income. The children of such women would most likely grow up in poor neighborhoods with inadequate parental supervision. These children are much more likely to turn to a life of crime.

Thus the potential greatness argument does not work. Sure, it would be bad to prevent a future MLK or a future Gandhi from being born, but these men—like most "great" people—did not grow up in poverty. It would also be bad, for the same kinds of reasons, to fail to prevent a future Charles Manson or John Wayne Gacy from coming to be. And there is good reason to think that unwanted fetuses are at least as likely to belong to the latter group as to the former. Thus it would be a good thing, on the average, to prevent such persons from coming to be. This "potential greatness" argument thus has a corollary: the "potential horribleness" argument. And if we allow the potential greatness of the fetus to be a factor in whether abortion is acceptable, then it seems we would have to equally allow the potential horribleness to be a factor. The result is that this line of thinking actually provides as much of an argument in favor of abortion as it does against abortion.

RIGHTS OF POTENTIAL PERSONS

There are, however, better versions of the potentiality argument that do not depend on the fetus's potential for greatness. Instead these arguments are based on the potential for the fetus simply to develop into a person. This type of argument does not appeal specifically to what kind of person the fetus will be but merely to the fact that it will, if it develops normally, eventually become a person. And one does not need to be a great person, or even a good person, to deserve moral consideration.

One version of this potential person argument would claim that the fetus has the same right to life as a fully developed person because the fetus is potentially a fully developed person. This claim implies that whatever moral obligations we have to a person like you or me, we have the same moral obligations to a potential person. On this view, what gives the potential person moral rights is not its potential to be a particular *kind* of person but more generally its potential to be a person *at all*. Presumably those who make this sort of argument are, at least implicitly, taking it to be an instance of a more general principle that if we have moral obligations to some X because it is an X, then we have the same obligations to any potential X because it will eventually be an X. For example, if we have a duty not to kill people (except in self-defense, etc.) because they are people, then we also have the same moral duty not to kill *potential* people (because they are potential *people*). But this more general principle is one that we should reject.

The problem with this more general principle is that, when applied to other potential things, it has crazy results; and if a principle can be used to derive something absurd, then the principle itself must be rejected or at least modified. For example, I think that innocent victims of crime deserve compensation. That is a reasonable claim, even if some disagree with it. But we are all potential victims. If a potential X has the same moral rights and entitlements as an actual X, then potential victims have the same rights and entitlements as actual victims. Thus, if every one of us is a potential victim, then every one of us deserves compensation. This, of course, is an absurd conclusion. Since the claim that victims deserve compensation is, by itself, reasonable, then it must be the principle (that a potential X deserves the same treatment as an actual X) that leads to the absurdity. Thus the principle must be rejected.

The pro-lifer who affirms the rights of potential persons might object that it is incorrect to say that we are all *potential* victims, or at least that we are potential victims in the same way that the fetus is a potential person. The fetus has the power within itself to develop into a person, given the proper conditions. And this process of becoming a person is part of its natural development that, to some degree, comes about automatically. But a person does not have *within himself* the power to become a victim (unless you want to say that there are suicide "victims"—but even so, they are not entirely *innocent* victims). Being a victim of a crime is something that happens to someone; it involves an outside cause. Also, becoming a victim is in no way automatic; it requires the agency of some third party. So it might be more accurate to say that we are all *possible* victims than to say we are potential victims. We are not naturally and automatically headed toward victimhood. (I will say more about the difference between potentiality and possibility later.)

But this does not save the potentiality principle, for we could draw other absurd conclusions from it. For example, I think that the elderly and infirm should have the right not to work. But we are all potentially elderly and infirm. This is not a mere possibility, something that might happen to us due to some external cause. It is the natural course of our human development. It would surely be absurd to say that we all have the right to retire and be cared for in our youth, while we are still able-bodied, just because we will in the future grow old. Similarly, we think that rational adults have the right to freedom of speech or freedom of religion. But we do not grant these same rights to children, even though they are potential adults. If a mother forces her eight-year-old child to go to church, she is surely not violating his right to freedom of religion. But if she were to force *me* to go to her church, then she would be violating my right to freedom of religion. I have that right as an adult, to go to whatever church I please (or not to go to any church, if I so please). The child does not have that right even though it is potentially an adult. Thus we should reject the claim that any potential X has the same rights as an actual X. If the fetus has a right to life, it cannot have this right simply on the basis of being a potential person. There needs to be a stronger argument.

ROBBING ONE'S FUTURE

A more sophisticated version of the potentiality argument was put forward by a philosopher named Don Marquis, in an article that now appears in nearly every applied ethics textbook that deals with the issue of abortion. Marquis refers to his version of the potentiality argument as the future-like-ours argument, because it is based on the fact that the fetus's future life, were it to have one, would be a life of the same sort as the life lived by a regular person like you or me, even though its life now is only biological. Though this future-like-ours argument is the product of professional philosophy, I think that arguments based on the fetus's potential get much of their intuitive force from this idea of a future like ours, even though the average nonphilosopher might not be able to articulate this notion as clearly as Marquis does.

The argument basically works this way. What makes it wrong to kill a person like you or me is that it robs her of her future. The reason why killing a person is wrong is not because it causes the victim pain or suffering, for painlessly killing an innocent person in her sleep would still be wrong even though the victim would not suffer any emotional anxiety or physical pain. Killing a person usually causes suffering to her family and friends who mourn the loss of their loved one. But this cannot be what makes killing an innocent person wrong, for then it would not be wrong to kill a hermit or a recluse who has no family or friends. Certainly being killed is bad for the victim, not just for others, and surely that is the main reason why we think it is wrong.

What makes it wrong to kill a person is that it denies that person of a future that has value to that person. But what kind of future is it that has value? It cannot be merely one's continued existence as a biological organism that has value. Suppose I expose someone to a poison that renders him permanently and irrevocably comatose without actually killing him. It seems to me that this would be as bad as murdering him. Most of us would be indifferent to being permanently comatose or biologically dead. Some people might even have a preference for being completely dead rather than being in the limbolike state of permanent unconsciousness. So this "future of value" is the future *conscious experiences* we would have. It is the combination of future activities, enjoyments, and decisions—all the things we do and experience—that is valuable to us. And it is the loss of all of these future conscious experiences that makes death a bad thing and the killing of innocent people morally wrong. This explains why we usually think of murdering someone as worse than torturing or raping someone. Torture might require greater cruelty, and those who torture and rape might be more evil than those who "merely" kill. Torture or rape might even cause more suffering to the victim than being killed. Nevertheless, when someone is tortured (and not killed) he can at least go on to live the rest of his life; the rape victim can at least have the opportunity to overcome her ordeal. It might require considerable struggle to get over the trauma, but at least there is the possibility of doing so. When someone is killed, he is denied all possible future experiences.

That is the first premise of the argument: What makes death bad is the loss of this future of conscious experiences. And what makes murder wrong is that the victim is robbed of this future. The second premise is that the fetus, if it is not aborted and no accident befalls it, has the same kind of future as you or I have. It has the same sort of life to look forward to as the rest of us do. Thus, since killing the fetus would be denying it the same kind of future experiences that you and I will have, it would be as wrong to kill the fetus as it would be wrong to kill you or me. The first premise is plausible and the second seems undeniable. But let us consider this argument a little more carefully.

I am inclined to agree that what would make my death a bad thing to *me*—as well as the reason it would be wrong for someone to kill me—is the loss of my future conscious experiences, which are of great value to me. But there remains an important question: does this future have value because I value it now? Or does it have value because it will be valued by the future me that will actually live through it? Put more simply, does my future life have value because I want to live or because my future self will be glad to be alive?

FUTURE HAS VALUE TO ME NOW

The pro-choice advocates would certainly favor the first account—that my future has value because I now desire to live out this future. And this is roughly the pro-choice argument given by philosopher Michael Tooley. This is surely very reasonable, as there are things that I want to do and experience in the future. I want to finish writing this book and eventually see it in print; I want to teach a class in Vienna as part of the university's study abroad program; I want to write another book; I want to vacation in the Caribbean next winter; and so on. I have plans and projects that I am engaged in. I have desires to have certain experiences in the future.

If it is our *current* desires for our conscious future life that gives that future its value, then the future-like-ours argument is not an affective argument against abortion because the fetus cannot have any current desire to live out its conscious future life. It has no projects or plans; it does not even have a conception of itself or the future and perhaps is not even capable of having any sorts of desires whatsoever. Thus if it is only our current desire to have future experiences that give that future value, then the fetus's future can have no value to it. Of course, it is possible for the fetus's future to have value to someone else, such as its parents, because they might desire its future. But this would only be an argument against involuntary or forced abortion, which both pro-lifers and pro-choicers would oppose.

One response that a pro-lifer might give to this problem is to insist that my future can have value to me now even if I do not desire it. This response takes two forms. (1) When I am asleep or passed out I cannot plan or desire the future, yet my future has value even at that time, even though I am unconscious. Thus, even though the fetus is not yet conscious of its future, that future can still have value. (2) If I were so severely depressed that I lost the desire to live, my future life could still have value because I will eventually get over my depression and be glad to be alive.

STANDING VERSUS OCCURRENT DESIRES

Let us consider the first pro-life response. If I am temporarily unconscious, I cannot desire my future, but it still has value, so the value of my future cannot depend entirely on my desire for it. There is surely some truth to this. My future does not lose any of its value to me when I take a nap. But that does not mean that the pro-choicers must deny that one's future having value depends on one now desiring to have that future. The problem with the no-desire-for-future-while-asleep argument is that it involves a very narrow notion of what it means to "desire" something.

Philosophers sometimes distinguish between what they call "occurrent" desires and "standing" desires. An *occurrent* desire is one that you actually feel at the moment. When I am thirsty I have an occurrent desire for water. When I daydream longingly about spending time in Paris, then I have an occurrent desire to vacation there. If I drink the water and satisfy my thirst, then the desire goes away. But the occurrent desire can also go away without being satisfied. If I stop thinking about Paris and get back to work writing this book, then I no longer have the occurrent desire to visit Paris.

My felt yearning for a vacation in Paris may go away because I am con-centrating on something else. Nevertheless, there is another sense in which I still do desire a vacation in Paris. This is what we mean by a *standing* desire. Standing desires are persistent and usually quite general desires that we con-tinue to have even when they are not felt. In what sense do I still desire to visit Paris? Whenever I think of Paris I want to go there; I work to save my money for the trip (even when I am not thinking about the vacation); if someone gave me a plane ticket to Paris, I would be very excited and grateful; and so on.

Think of very general desires, such as the desire to have a successful career, or to be a good parent, or to lose weight. We continue to have these desires, and continue to act accordingly, even during those times when we are not thinking about them. Surely if you said to me that "Sally desires to have children someday," and I reply, "You are wrong; she has no such desire because she is asleep right now," you would probably think I was merely trying to be difficult. She has a standing desire to have kids, even if right now she does not feel that yearning to be a mother.

If it were not for standing desires, we would have a hard time being properly motivated to do much of anything except satisfy our most imme-diate cravings. I study because I desire to be a good philosopher. But if I could not continue having this desire even when I am not thinking about my career, then as soon as I focus on the article I am reading, I would no longer have the desire to be a good scholar. But without the desire to be a good scholar, I would no longer have any reason to read the boring article.

In response to the argument that the fetus's future has no value to it because it cannot desire its future, the pro-life reply is that an unconscious person's future can have value, and thus so can a not-yet-conscious fetus's future. The problem we can now see with this reply is that it seems to assume that all desires are occurrent desires and that there are no standing desires (or that only occurrent desires can give the desired object value, which is equally mistaken). It is mostly standing desires that give our future its value to us. It is not so much my fleeting and transient occurrent desires that give my future value, for these desires will often vanish well before they could be satisfied. After a frustrating day at the university I might have a passing whim to give up philosophy, move to Florida, and become a scuba instructor. Acting on that desire would probably not be a good idea. What gives one's future most of its value are those broad standing desires, such as the desire to get a degree, have a successful career, raise a family, or retire early.

All standing desires will occasionally be occurrent desires. It would not make sense to say that Sally desires to have children if she never once felt a certain longing for the "pitter patter of tiny feet." She may not feel it often, but she has to feel it at least once in a while. Thus my future continues to have value for me even when I am asleep because I continue to have a standing desire for it. The fetus, on the other hand, has no desires for its future or things in its future, neither standing nor occurrent. The value of our future can depend on our (standing) desires for it, but the fetus's future can have no value because it can have no desire for it.

DESIRING ONE'S ACTUAL FUTURE VERSUS DESIRING ONE'S PERCEIVED FUTURE

The second pro-life response to the claim that our future has value only because we desire it is that the future life of someone who is severely depressed and has lost the desire to live can still have value for that person. Suppose my friend Bill is suffering from severe depression, and thus his projects seem doomed to fail, his dreams and hopes for the future seem to him to be certain to remain unfulfilled, and he feels that he has nothing to look forward to. Bill might not value his future and he might be indifferent to the prospect of dying soon. Now let us suppose that Bill's depression is temporary and his life is not hopeless. He still has considerable talent, and with some effort he can get his life back on track. Eventually he will enjoy life again and will have projects that he believes in and that will have a decent chance of success. If one's future has value only because one desires it now, then Bill's future has no value (to him), no matter how good it might be, because he does not now, in his depressed state, have any desire—standing or occurrent—to live out this future. The pro-lifer could say that since Bill's future clearly does have value (for Bill), then we must reject the claim that someone's future has value only because that person desires to have those future conscious experiences. If Bill's future can have value even though he does not desire it, then perhaps the fetus's future can have value even though it cannot desire it.

There is, however, a major difference between the value of Bill's life to Bill, and the value of the fetus's life to the fetus. One important difference, it seems to me, is that, even though Bill does not desire his future, he is *capable* of desiring it. He can conceive of himself in the future and has desires and hopes. The fetus, on the other hand, is not capable of having desires or of having any conception of the future.

Why is this difference so important? Well, for one, Bill may not desire his future *as he perceives it to be*, but his perception is skewed by his depression. Furthermore, he still has some desires. He must have a desire that his projects succeed, otherwise he would not be bothered by the thought of his projects failing. Bill desires to have a successful career, to be happily married, to have friends. It is because he believes (falsely) that his future will lack these things that he has no desire for it. Bill *does* desire a future in which his career prospects suddenly improve and his love life gets more satisfying. But he does not care about experiencing what he thinks will be his actual future.

If Bill's future has value, how would I, as his friend, convince him of that? I would try to show him that his future is not as bleak as he perceives it to be. I would try to convince him that he does (or will) have better career prospects than he realizes, that his love life can improve, and so on. If I am right, and Bill's future does potentially contain these qualities that he desires, then Bill does desire his *actual* future—the things that he wants to do and experience are things that can or will happen in his future. It is only his inaccurate image of the future that he has no desire to live through.

Suppose, on the other hand, that Bill's future life *was* doomed to be miserable. Suppose that, on top of all the problems he has now, he will soon come down with a terminal illness that will cause him so much pain that he will be unable to enjoy the few remaining activities and pleasures of life, such as good food and pleasant company. He will get little or no reprieve from the pain until he dies. It seems reasonable for Bill to want to avoid this future and that it in fact has no value (at least not to him). If he were hit and killed by a bus tomorrow, he might be better off, since at least he would have been spared the pointless suffering caused by his terminal illness.

The moral of the story? To say that something is valuable to a person does not require that the person actually desire it. We can desire or fail to desire something due to some error in belief or perception. We can desire something that is not valuable or (as with Bill's case) fail to desire something that is valuable because we fail to see what is desirable about it. The critic of the future-like-ours argument against abortion can thus modify his claim that the value of our future depends on us desiring it. For my future to have value I need not actually desire it, but it must be a future that I should desire and would desire if I were made aware of it. My future does not require that I actually desire to live through what I think will be my future experiences, but it does require that I have *some* desires. It must promise the fulfillment of at least some of the desires that I have now.

This pro-choice line of defense against the future-like-ours argument may appear to the pro-lifer to be mere sophistry, a game with words. Couldn't we say that the fetus would certainly desire its future if it could be made aware of it and if it were able to desire? Not really. We need to have some real desires for anything to be valuable to us. And different people desire different things. For example, suppose Bill's future contains a life involving fame and success and wealth, but it is destined to be a lonely life with no family and few close friends. How much value does this successful-but-lonely future have for Bill? Well, that is going to depend a lot on what Bill actually desires, what hopes and dreams he has. If Bill always dreamed of being rich and famous and tended to be a bit of a loner, then this would be the ideal life for him. He should desire this future; and in a sense he already does desire this future. If, on the other hand, Bill never cared much for material success but finds joy only in warm personal relations, then this future has considerably less value to him. There is little of what he desires to be found in his future experiences and much of what he does not desire. Since the fetus as of yet has no desires, no plans or projects or preferences, we cannot say what, if any, value its future conscious experiences have for it now.

FUTURE DESIRES FOR OUR FUTURE

Maybe we have been looking at this future-of-value thing all wrong. Maybe we are right to say that in order for future conscious experiences to have value for a person, that person must desire to have certain conscious experiences that are included in that future. But perhaps the mistake was in thinking that, for a certain future to have value to me, I must have some desire *now* for certain conscious experiences. This is the problem faced by the pro-life side because the fetus cannot now have any desire for future experiences. The pro-lifer could insist that for my future to have value to me, I do not have to desire it now. Perhaps all that is required is for me to desire it at some point in the future. This seems more reasonable. After all, suppose that I now desire a future of fame and success even if it requires forsaking friends and sacrificing intimate relationships. In a few years hence, however, my preferences and plans will drastically change, and I will find such a life shallow and vain. I will come to strongly prefer a life that is more ordinary but that includes warm friendships and a loving wife. (Let us suppose that these new desires will not change again but will persist for the rest of my life.) Which future would be better for me? The lonely, successful life, which I prefer now but will not prefer when it arrives? Certainly not. The future that would be better for me is the one that I will prefer *at that time I am experiencing it*.

If this interpretation of the future-of-value is correct, then it seems possible that the fetus's future has value even though it does not have any desires now. Its future can have value (to the fetus itself, or at least to the person that it will become) because it will, at some point in the future, have a desire to have conscious experiences further in the future.

HOW MUCH VALUE DOES THE FETUS'S FUTURE HAVE?

Let us assume, for the sake of argument, that the fetus's future life has value to it, and that what makes death a bad thing is the loss of this future. We still need to ask two questions: (1) How much should we be obligated to value the fetus's future life? (Does it have enough value such that abortion is always, or even usually, wrong?) And (2) is the fetus in any way entitled to its future?

Let us start with question (1). How much are we obligated to value the fetus's future life? Just because the fetus's future is similar to ours, and it has some value, that does not necessarily mean that its future has the same value (or should be valued as much) as ours. To put this more generally, just because two things both have value, and have value for the same reason, does not mean that they have the same value or should be valued the same.

Consider the case of Dr. Smith, a seventy-eight-year-old woman who is still active, working as a semiretired fertility expert in an in vitro fertilization clinic. One night she is alone in the lab thawing a frozen embryo that she is planning to implant into the uterus of a hopeful mother the next day. There are no other people in the lab and no other embryos either. A fire breaks out and quickly spreads throughout the clinic. At about that time I happen to be walking by on my way home from the pub. Being the heroic fellow that I am, I charge into the burning clinic to find the embryo in a large, heavy insulating device and poor Dr. Smith unconscious on the floor. I can save only one— which one should it be, the embryo or the doctor? Let us assume, for the sake of simplicity, that the doctor has no children or close relatives, and that most of her friends have either passed on or moved to Florida. (This way we can ignore the suffering of other people who know her, which we will assume would not be any greater than the disappointment that the parents would feel at having to wait longer to have their first child.) Since Dr. Smith is already unconscious, we can also ignore any pain or fear that she might experience; if left inside the building she will die peacefully from smoke inhalation before her body is consumed by fire. If we consider Dr. Smith's future and the embryo's future to be of comparable value, then I should probably save the embryo, since it has so much more future. The embryo has probably around seventy years ahead of itself, whereas Dr. Smith is already very old. Even if very healthy, she cannot realistically hope for much more than ten years. (If the embryo's future is of the same qualitative value, then its greater quantity should outweigh the relatively small quantity of time that the doctor has remaining ahead of her.)

The future-of-value argument for abortion thus seems to have the very counterintuitive implication that the life of a fetus can have more value than the life of a fully developed person. I myself would not hesitate to save the doctor and would not take even a small risk in going back for the embryo.

Moreover, if someone else were to have arrived on the scene and saved the embryo instead, leaving Dr. Smith to perish in the conflagration, I would think that person to have committed a grave moral error. I suppose this is simply my intuition. Our gut reactions to cases like this are certainly no guarantee of the truth, and other people might not share these intuitions. But I suspect that most people who are honest and think critically about such a case would agree that we should certainly save the doctor. Only a pro-life fanatic would prefer the life of a frozen embryo over the life of a person. If someone insists that we should save the embryo and let the doctor die, then we may have reached a point where we simply cannot continue this discussion.

It is important not to end this discussion with a mere appeal to intuition, for our intuition might be the result of biases or other sorts of irrational thinking. So what exactly explains my intuition—which I hope you share— that the doctor's life (with its relatively short future) is much more worth preserving then is the embryo's life (despite its much longer future)? The embryo has only its *future* desires to live out its future conscious experiences. It will have desires and plans and projects that will give its future life value. Dr. Smith, however, has *actual* desires and plans right now for her future. She has fewer future desires, since her future is so short, while the embryo has many more future desires, since it still has so much of its future ahead of it. But the doctor's few present desires for her future gives her future a value that far exceeds the value that the embryo's future has at this time. Her current plans and projects give her short future more value than the embryo's future plans and projects give its long future. There is no absurdity in claiming that the value we should place on someone's future can increase in time just as it might also decrease over time.

So where does that leave us with regard to the issue of abortion? Even if we agree that we should value the future life of the doctor much more highly than the future life of the embryo, that does not mean that the future life of the embryo has *no* value, only that it has *less* value than the future life of a fully developed, actual person like you or me. For all that, it might still be that the embryo's future life has *some* value. Suppose Mrs. Smith were able to save herself, plus one item from the burning clinic, and she chose to save her beloved bonsai tree instead of the embryo. Maybe we would be right to disapprove of that decision. It might also be that this value that the embryo's life has—however small compared to mine or yours—is enough to make it wrong to deny it of this future. If so, then this could be enough to make abortion wrong except when continued pregnancy threatens the life of the pregnant mother.

IS THE FETUS (EMBRYO) ENTITLED TO ITS FUTURE?

Let us now consider the second question we asked earlier. Does the fact that the fetus's life has some value to it—or to the future person it will become—mean that it would be wrong to deny it this future? Just because something has value to someone does not mean that the person is entitled to it. By analogy, an endowed chair at the University of Michigan would be of great value to me, but the University of Michigan has every right to deny me this position. I have not earned it and was never promised it. Similarly, the pro-choicer could argue that, even if the fetus's life has value to it, that does not mean the fetus is entitled to its life. This analogy, of course, is not perfect. For one thing, giving the position to me would require denying it to someone else (actually, to everyone else, including people who are more deserving of it than I am). Denying the fetus its future, by contrast, would not (under normal circumstances) deprive anyone else of their future conscious experiences. Furthermore, the University of Michigan's endowed chair position is not mine in any meaningful sense, so I have no claim on it. But the fetus's future certainly is *its* future in some seemingly significant sense. It cannot be lived by anyone else.

Of course, we could try to make the analogy closer. Perhaps there is some false or misleading piece of information on a worker's evaluation by his boss. Maybe the information is damning; maybe it is undeservedly praising. This information could be very valuable to the worker in several ways. If the information is bad, he can do things to indicate that it is not true. For example, if the information implies that he does not put in a full forty hours per week, then he can make it a point to be seen working before nine and after five. If the information is good, he might try to use it to leverage for a wage increase. Granting the worker this information would not deprive anyone else of anything of value. And it is his information, *his* performance evaluation. But is he entitled to it? While it might seem unfair for the worker to be unable to correct false claims on his evaluation, the company can say that it needs the evaluation process to remain confidential to ensure that supervisors are frank. If the worker had a right to this information, then the company would be obligated to show it to him no matter how good the reasons are for confidentiality.

So, just because the fetus's life has some value to it (or to the future person it will become) does not automatically mean that it has any right or entitlement to it. The pro-lifer might say that this is a bad analogy. I might not be entitled to every piece of information about me, but surely I am entitled to my life and to my future! My future life is not just one good thing among others. Other good things are subject to trade-offs. The worker might be willing to work in a place that has secret evaluations if it pays more than another job with more open evaluations. There is no such trade-off with my future life. But this is not entirely true. We often trade off part of our future life for other goods, as when we do not try to quit smoking even though we know that will mean that our future life is a little shorter. But of course, in that case, it is the smoker who is freely trading off part of her future for the pleasures of smoking. It would be wrong for *us* to trade off some of *her* future for some other good (even for what we think is a good thing for her).

Still, if you do not think that it would be OK to save the embryo over Dr. Smith, then it is not clear that the embryo is entitled to its future life, at least not in the same way that Dr. Smith is entitled to her future. If both were entitled to their future, then we would have to flip a coin. If you think that we should save Dr. Smith, then you do not think that the embryo is entitled to its future.

SUGGESTED FURTHER READING

Cudd, Ann. "Sensationalized Philosophy: A Reply to Marquis's 'Why Abortion Is Immoral.'" *Journal of Philosophy* 87 (1990): 262–64.

Marquis, Don. "Why Abortion Is Immoral." *Journal of Philosophy* 86 (1989): 183–202.

McInerney, Peter. "Does a Fetus Already Have a Future?" *Journal of Philosophy* 87 (1990): 264–68.

Norcross, Alastair. "Killing, Abortion, and Contraception." *Journal of Philosophy* 87 (1990): 268–77.

Sinnott-Armstrong, Walter. "You Can't Lose What You Ain't Never Had." *Philosophical Studies* 96 (1999): 59–72.

Tooley, Michael. "Abortion and Infanticide." *Philosophy and Public Affairs* (1972): 37–65.

CHAPTER 7

THE GOLDEN RULE ARGUMENT AGAINST ABORTION

Many people, when faced with a difficult moral dilemma, appeal to the good old-fashioned "golden rule"—a moral principle that is found in the teachings of Jesus, the Buddha, and Confucius, among others. This rule, as formulated in the King James version of the New Testament, tells us to "do unto others as we would have them do unto us." The appeal to the golden rule is useful because it avoids difficult questions such as whether or not the fetus has a soul or whether potential persons have moral rights. By applying a certain version of the golden rule to the abortion issue, maybe we can come to some conclusion regarding the morality of abortion without dealing with these sorts of highly disputed questions. It also has strong intuitive appeal. Some philosophers, such as R. M. Hare and Harry Gensler, have used the golden rule (or something like it) to make an argument against abortion. Many nonphilosophers come to have moral disapproval of abortion by first feeling thankful that they themselves had not been aborted. "I would not want to have been aborted," they think to themselves, "so I cannot say that it is OK for someone else to have an abortion."

STANDARD VERSION OF THE GOLDEN RULE

Let's start with a straightforward application of the golden rule. On a standard reading, the golden rule commands us to do to others what we would prefer they do to us. This can be legitimately extended to the command that we should do to others what we are glad was done to us. This extension to past actions involves merely altering "as you would *have* them do" to "as you would *have had* them do." A more precise, tenseless version of this could be couched in terms of what you would prefer in hypothetical situations. When considering the morality of abortion, I should suppose that it is not some particular woman now contemplating terminating her pregnancy but my own mother in the past deciding whether or not to terminate the pregnancy that would actually result in me. Could I say, "Go ahead; feel free to have an abortion"? One reason for thinking that I might have to say, "No, don't do it" is that if she had had the abortion, then I would not now have been born. I would disapprove of an abortion that would result in my never having existed, so I cannot approve of other abortions (since they would similarly result in a future person not existing).

PROBLEMS WITH THE GOLDEN RULE AND REFORMULATION

The traditional golden rule has its problems. For one, what if I like it when people say mean and insulting things to me? Maybe I am a masochist, or maybe it inspires me to work harder. If I should treat others in the same way that I like to be treated, then I should say mean and insulting things to other people. This seems counterintuitive. Or what if I am very wealthy and do not want help from others. That would mean, on a standard interpretation of the golden rule, that I should avoid helping other people. Furthermore, if someone less fortunate than me would prefer to be helped, then he is obligated to help others. In this way the traditional golden rule leads to a strange sort of relativism.

Gensler, along with some other philosophers, argue for a new and improved version of the golden rule that avoids these problems. This new, formal version of the golden rule can be derived from two basic and plausible rational requirements on moral judgments, the "universalizability" principle and the "prescriptivity" principle. The *universalizability* principle goes like this:

> If you think it is morally permissible to do something to someone, then you
> must think that it would be morally permissible for others to do the same
> thing to you in similar circumstances.

According to this principle we must make similar judgments about similar
cases. If you make two different moral judgments about two similar cases,
then you must be able to point out some morally relevant difference between
the two. The fact that in one case one person is affected and in the other case
another person is affected is not by itself a morally relevant difference. I
think any reasonable person would have to accept that. The *prescriptivity*
principle goes like this:

> If you think that it would be morally permissible for someone to do a cer-
> tain action to you, then you must consent to the idea of someone doing that
> act to you.

This is simply to say that moral judgments are about what people should or
should not do—they express our approval or disapproval. While the universalizability principle is a demand of consistency among relevantly similar
moral beliefs, the prescriptivity principle is a demand of consistency
between moral beliefs and corresponding attitudes, motivation, or actions.

The principles of universalizability and prescriptivity can be combined
to derive a formal version of the golden rule:

> If you think that it would be morally permissible to do a certain act to
> someone, then you must consent to the idea of someone doing the same act
> to you (in similar circumstances).

This version of the golden rule is a demand for consistency between moral
judgments and motivation or action. Unlike the familiar golden rule "Do
unto others as you would have them do unto you," this version of the golden
rule is not a moral principle. It is a principle not for governing our behavior
but for governing our moral reasoning.

The fact that I cannot consent to the idea of someone doing a certain act
to me, combined with the formal golden rule, requires me to conclude that it
is not acceptable for me to do that action to someone else (in a similar situation). For example, I would greatly resent the idea of someone robbing my
house when I am out of town. Combined with the formal golden rule, this

attitude forces me to hold that it is not morally acceptable for me to rob my neighbor's house when he is away. I could steal from my neighbor without remorse and be consistent if I were to change my attitudes about others stealing from me. I could change my attitudes and become more accepting of the idea and give my consent. But this is not a realistic option. I could *say*, "Go ahead and rob my house"—but I would not really be OK with it. For this reason, we cannot derive moral obligations from the formal golden rule alone. However, we can criticize someone's moral judgments by using the formal golden rule to show that she is inconsistent. Furthermore, the formal golden rule can be combined with facts about our attitudes and preferences to yield moral judgments that we must accept on pain of contradiction.

One problem with the traditional golden rule is that it seems to rely on having the proper attitudes to begin with. For example, I might in fact have no objections to others refusing to help me with their charity and keeping all their wealth for themselves. After all, I am doing reasonably well. I have no need for their help. Thus it might seem that I could consistently judge that I have no duty to help the poor. But we must remember that the golden rule says that, however I think I should act with respect to others, I must consent to the same thing being done to me *in a similar situation*. So the question is whether I could maintain this attitude in a situation of desperate need. Would I have no objections to other people spending all of their money on frivolous luxuries, or saving their money like misers, in a situation where I am starving from lack of food? Probably not. So I cannot consistently believe that it is OK for me not to help them. This helps to solve part of the traditional golden rule's problem of relativism. It does not depend on the circumstances of who is applying the golden rule as much as it does the circumstances of those to whom it is being applied.

Another objection to the traditional golden rule is that it might lead to absurd results because there are many things that we might believe not to be morally wrong but that we nevertheless would not like being done to us. For example, suppose I give an F to a student who does significantly substandard work. The standard reading of the golden rule implies that since I would not want an F, I must think it is wrong for me to give such a grade to the student. This result is clearly incorrect. It seems that it is not only morally acceptable for me to assign an F for significantly substandard work, but it might even be my duty as a professor to assign the grade that the student deserves. To do otherwise would be unfair to other students.

The formal version of the golden rule solves this problem. For one, the formal golden rule does not apply simply to what I am or am not willing to consent to. Would I consent to receiving an F if I were the student? Probably not, but I also would probably not do substandard work if I were the student. I must ask myself what I would consent to *in a similar situation*. Would I consent to receiving an F if I were in the student's place and, like the student, had done substandard work? I believe that I would be willing to receive the F in that situation.

The other improvement is that the formal golden rule requires only that I must *consent* to being given an F; it does not require that I *want* an F. There are many things we can consent to that we would not like. If I play a game of chess, I consent to losing if my opponent outplays me. (It would certainly be no fun if he let me win.) But that does not mean that I want to lose. I would not welcome an F, and I might hope that the instructor would give me a passing grade even though I did not deserve it (either due to miscalculation or out of pity), but I would still *consent* to the F—assuming that I did not dispute the professor's assessment of the quality of my work. I might be unhappy with the F, but I would not object or feel that I was wronged. The student registered for the class knowing that he would be graded on his performance. If the student would not consent to being given an F for substandard work, then he would have found the policy objectionable at that time.

MEETING OBJECTIONS TO THE FORMAL GOLDEN RULE

The first, perhaps most obvious objection that the pro-choicer might give to the golden rule argument against abortion is that, by applying the formal golden rule to the abortion issue, we are already assuming that the fetus is a person, an assumption the pro-choicer would not accept. If you judge that it is morally OK to do a particular act *to someone* then you must consent to the idea of someone doing the same act to you. But this follows only if the "someone" being acted on is a person, like you. In some sense this is correct. I might, for example, think that it is morally permissible to kill and eat a pig, but that does not commit me to consenting to the idea of someone killing *me* for food. The formal golden rule claims that if I judge an action to be OK, then I must accept the same thing being done to me in a similar situation. But there are important differences between a pig and me.

The criticism is off the mark because it takes the formal golden rule too literally. It is perfectly reasonable to insist that for an action to be a morally right or wrong it must affect persons somehow. Nevertheless, there are many ways to affect someone without acting on that person directly, such as burning down his house. My neighbor's house is not a person. Yet I must admit that it would be wrong to burn it down—not because it would commit me to consenting to the idea of other people burning *me* down, but because it would commit me to consenting to the idea of someone burning my house down. The same applies to the fetus. In applying the formal golden rule to abortion I must ask not whether I consent to having been aborted when *I was* a fetus, but whether or not I can consent to the aborting of the fetus that *was to become me*. This does not require me to think of the fetus as a person like myself any more than the previous example requires that I think of my neighbor's house as a person.

Another, more serious objection to the golden rule antiabortion argument is that it does not make any sense to talk about consenting to past events or actions. This objection, however, fails to take into account that the formal golden rule requires us to ask what we now consent to for some hypothetical situation, not necessarily what we consent to regarding our present situation. Thus the case to be considered is not the actual case in which I have already been born, but a hypothetical one in which I have not yet been born and might conceivably be aborted. I must ask what I could consent to regarding the decision of my mother back when she was still pregnant with the fetus that would become me. But of course, it is not what I would consent to if I were *in* that hypothetical situation, because in the hypothetical situation either I am the fetus—and thus incapable of having any opinion or preference on the matter—or I am capable of giving advice to the woman—and then I am not the fetus (or certainly not an ordinary fetus!). The question we must consider is what we now, in the actual world, consent to for the hypothetical world.

The final objection is one that pro-choicers raise against many antiabortion arguments. If the formal golden rule commits us to the claim that abortion is wrong, then it also commits us to the claim that contraception and even abstinence are equally morally wrong. If I think that it is OK for people to avoid pregnancy, then I must consent to my mother having avoided the pregnancy that resulted in me. I cannot consent to that because then I never would have existed. This is clearly absurd; there is certainly nothing morally objectionable in avoiding pregnancy. So there must be something wrong with the golden rule, at least when applied to issues of reproduction.

The defender of the golden rule argument against abortion could make a similar response to the one that might be given in defense of other antiabortion arguments. A distinction must be made between *potential* persons and mere *possible* persons. A potential person is a real, actually existing entity with the power of developing into a person under proper conditions. A merely possible person, on the other hand, does not exist, but perhaps it could exist. Abstaining from sex or using contraception does not cause the nonexistence of anything, for there is nothing acted on. Abortion involves acting on some existing thing, a thing that has the power to develop into a person. It may be questionable as to whether and to what extent potential persons have moral rights, but no one would grant rights to merely *possible* persons. The golden rule states that if you think it is morally acceptable to do a certain action to someone, then you must consent to the idea of someone doing that same act to you. The action need not be directly acting on a person, but it needs to be acting on *something*.

Of course, the pro-choicer might continue to push this objection, claiming that the distinction between possible persons and potential persons is not relevant from the point of view of the formal golden rule. If the status of the fetus (i.e., whether it has a soul, or whether potential persons have rights, etc.) does not matter for the golden rule argument, then whatever acts or omissions would lead to my nonexistence is something that I could not consent to and therefore must morally oppose on pain of contradiction.

Of course, there are some things you could consent to even though they might entail your nonexistence (or things you would refuse to consent to even though required for your existence). For example, suppose that Nelson's conception was the result of his mother being raped. Surely he would not consent to her having been raped, even though if she were not raped, Nelson would not have been born. The fact that Nelson was glad he was born does not commit him to consent to his mother having been raped. But, although this reasoning allows someone to consent to abstinence even though it might mean that that person would never have been born, at the same time it seems to weaken the use of the golden rule in the abortion issue. If I can approve of contraception even though I would not exist had my mother used it, then why can't I approve of abortion even though I would not exist had my mother taken that option?

The importance of the distinction between merely *possible* persons (who are denied existence by contraception) and *potential* persons (who are denied becoming persons by abortion) can be shown by applying the golden rule to the example of knowingly causing a fetus to have birth defects. Suppose a pregnant woman takes a drug that she knows will cause her fetus to become blind (and that has no beneficial effects on the fetus or the mother). It seems obviously wrong for the woman to take such a drug, and the golden rule would probably require that we disapprove of such acts. I could not judge that it is OK for her to take the drug because I would not consent to my mother having taken the drug (for then I would have been born blind).

Now consider a different case. A husband and wife, who are carriers for a genetic defect that causes blindness, try to conceive a child, knowing that it is highly likely that it will be born blind. I do not think that the golden rule requires that I disapprove of knowingly conceiving a child that will have a disability. Although I may prefer being able to see over being blind, I would prefer being blind over not existing at all. Although some might insist that the second case is morally wrong, this would be a rather controversial position, whereas the wrongness of intentionally causing the birth defect to an otherwise healthy fetus is not at all controversial. The difference in our intuitions is at least partly explained by the distinction between potential and possible persons. The first case involves acting on an actual entity with the potential to see, whereas the second case involves only a possible entity with no potential to see. The blinding of the fetus example supports the distinction between potential persons (such as fetuses) and merely possible persons (the child that the couple might conceive, if they have sex without contraception). And this allows the golden rule to be applied to abortion (potential people) but not abstinence or contraception (merely possible people).

INDETERMINACY OF POTENTIAL PERSONS

Let us limit the application of the golden rule to actions that affect existing things (persons, potential persons, etc.) and not mere possible things that do not actually exist (such as the fetus that could have been conceived had a couple not abstained). There still seems to be a problem—not for the formal golden rule itself, but with applying the golden rule to the contingent existence of particular future people. The problem arises due to the indeterminacy of potential people. A potential person is not potentially any one particular future person but is potentially a range of distinctly different future persons. Similarly, when we talk of a child as having "athletic potential" we do not think that, if encouraged, this junior athlete will definitely be a relief pitcher for the Chicago White Sox. Athletic potential can develop in a range of different ways; maybe the child will become a baseball pitcher or maybe a football quarterback. Athletic potential is not necessarily a destiny for a particular sport, let alone for a particular position, and certainly not for a particular team. Insofar as a potential is undeveloped it is also, to that extent, indeterminate. In other words, it is open to a wide range of distinct possibilities.

Thus, there is no one particular future person who is robbed of existence in an abortion, just as the White Sox could not complain that they were robbed of a future star pitcher simply because some athletic eight-year-old let his talent for sports go to waste while he pursued his interest in music. Because of this indeterminacy of potential, the golden rule has implications that are strongly counterintuitive when applied to potential persons. It seems to commit us to objecting to actions that are obviously morally permissible. There are many nonobjectionable actions—adoption in particular—that you might fail to consent to being done to the fetus that became you. I will illustrate this with a personal anecdote.

I was adopted at birth. Since I was adopted, I was presumably the result of an unwanted pregnancy. Thus abortion was, as far as I know, a real possibility for the fetus that became me. Given that I, unlike most people, could have actually been aborted, does that require me to be morally opposed to abortion?

When I was about twenty-eight years old, I was contacted by an investigator who told me that my biological family was searching for me. I decided to let them contact me—partly to reassure them that I turned out OK, partly out of curiosity to see to what degree genetic makeup determines personality, and partly with the hope that they might be fabulously wealthy. As a test case for the "nature versus nurture" debate, my experience was especially interesting because my biological parents eventually married each other and had two daughters. Thus I had two full-blooded sisters. Eventually I met my biological mother, father, paternal and maternal aunts, paternal and maternal grandmothers, and my two biological sisters. I quickly discovered that I had nothing in common with any of them apart from a few odd quirks. As it turns out, my biological mother and both sisters are strict fundamentalist Christians who do not believe in science or evolution (let alone philosophy).

Inevitably I was struck with the question of what would have happened to me, or the baby that eventually became me, had I not been given up for adoption. There are, of course, immediate circumstances that would have been different for the baby and the young child. But the more profound speculation is about how differently my upbringing would have been and how differently I would have turned out. What, or who, would I have become had I been raised by my birth mother rather than being adopted? For one thing, it is very unlikely that the person I would have become would be anything like the person I actually turned out to be. After all, my two biological sisters are more similar to me genetically than any other people on the planet, yet they share none of my interests, and their values and worldview could hardly be more different from mine. The same is true for all of my biological relatives. It seems most likely that, had I been raised by my biological parents, I would be very much like my sisters, or at least much more so than I am now, since I would then share very similar genes *and* a very similar environment growing up.

When I think about the person I would have become had I not been adopted, I find it very difficult to think of this person as *me*. For the sake of clarity I will refer to this person as "Glenn," assuming that this is the name the baby would have been given by my biological mother had she kept me (him). Glenn would, of course, have the same genes and so would probably look more or less like me, though he might have a different hairstyle, for example. But Glenn would probably think and act very differently from me. He would probably not be a professional philosopher. He would also have different friends and would engage in different activities and conversations with them. Most important, he would have a very different set of life experiences.

When we apply the formal golden rule to my situation, we get strongly counterintuitive results. Were I now able to give advice to my biological mother back when she was making the difficult decision of whether to keep the fetus that would become me, I would strongly advise her to give me up. I could not consent to her keeping me, for that would mean that I would not exist as surely as had I never been conceived. If she kept and raised the baby herself, then *someone* would exist (Glenn), someone with my genetic makeup, but it would not be me in any meaningful sense. According to the formal golden rule, this would commit me to the claim that it is not morally permissible for someone in the same position as my biological mother not to give her child up for adoption. But this is absurd. Obviously there is nothing morally wrong in principle with a woman raising her own biological children. It might be wrong in certain unusual instances, as in the case of drastically unfit parents. But it would be hard to argue that in this case.

Furthermore, had the baby who was to become me not been given up for adoption and grew up to become Glenn, Glenn would not realistically be able to consent to the baby that became him having been given up for adoption. But this seems to lead to a contradiction: it would be wrong for my biological mother to give her baby up for adoption from Glenn's point of view and wrong for her *not* to give up her baby from *my* point of view. If we cannot reliably apply the formal golden rule to the treatment of the newborn baby (in the case of adoption) because of the indeterminacy of potential, then it does not seem any more likely that we could apply it to the treatment of the fetus (in the case of abortion) for the same reasons.

THE VALUE OF ONE'S PERSONAL EXISTENCE

Those on the pro-life side might disagree with the claim that if I had been raised by different parents I would not exist, and so the application of the golden rule to abortion is very different from its application to adoption. But the problem with applying the golden rule to the abortion issue is not that Glenn and I are different people. The formal golden rule is about what I could reasonably consent to, and thus even if he is the same person as I am, Glenn would not consent to having been given up for adoption, and I would not consent to having been kept by my birth mother. The question depends not on whether we are the same person in some strange sense but rather on how I conceive of myself and what it is in my existence and my sense of self that I value and would not be willing to give up for any amount of compensation.

Perhaps we are determined by our genetic makeup, and so Glenn and I would have turned out just about the same regardless of environmental factors. Does that mean that I could consent to the fetus that became me becoming Glenn instead? I admit that what drew me to ask who I would have been had I not been adopted was, at least partially, my doubts about genetic determinism. However, the objection to the golden rule argument does not rely on any claims about personality being determined more by environment than by biology. It is possible that the potential person who was to become me might have developed in very much the same way had he grown up with different parents. Maybe Glenn would have turned out to be almost exactly like me in every way. He might have come to resemble me so closely in appearance, personality, and behavior that even my friends and family— were they to find themselves in this parallel universe in which I was not adopted—would not be able to distinguish Glenn from me (without asking specific details about his life, such as the names of family members or the elementary school that he attended).

Nevertheless, no matter how closely Glenn resembled me, I would not consider him to be the same person that I consider myself to be because he has lived a different life. Much of who I am and who I conceive myself to be is constituted by these specific details of my life. This is because the events and experiences that make up the narrative of my life are essentially constitutive of my personal sense of self.

In order to judge whether or not I (or Glenn) could reasonably consent to having been raised by different parents, we must ask what it is that Glenn and I share in common—and more important, what we do not share. What things about what I value in my existence would be lost had I grown up in a different family? Then we must ask which, if any, of these is what we value in our own personal existence.

One thing that Glenn and I share is our mere existence. Of course, Glenn and I do not both exist, but one of us would exist. In other words, if the baby were adopted by my parents, then I would exist; and similarly if the baby were raised by its natural parents, then Glenn would exist. No matter whether I am adopted or raised by my birth parents, there is someone who will exist. If it worked, this would save the golden rule argument against abortion, because this is an important difference between abortion and adoption; if the fetus is aborted then no one exists—not me, not Glenn, nobody.

But mere existence is something I share not just with Glenn but with every actual person. Surely what I value in my life is not that *someone* exists but rather something more personal and unique to me. Furthermore, if this was what was valuable in my life (that *someone* exists), then the formal golden rule would not require me to disapprove of abortion as long as the woman who aborts her fetus later goes on to have another child to make up for the one that she aborted, thus ensuring that there would still be someone who exists. Abortion opponents who appeal to the golden rule do not disapprove of abortion because there is one less person existing in the universe but because someone in particular is robbed of existence.

More than our mere existence, Glenn and I share an identical genetic code, and this is something that is unique to him and/or me and not shared by anyone else. It is shared by all the people that the fetus that became me might have become, but not by any other people (assuming I have no identical twins or clones). Certainly this cannot be what I value in my existence. I do not even know the slightest thing about my particular genetic code. Even if I got a complete analysis of my genetic code, it would be nothing more than an exhausting list of Ts, As, Cs, and Gs, the ordering of which would be of no significance to me.

Well, of course it is not the genes themselves that I value in my existence but all of the properties and character traits that these genes express, and this is something that Glenn and I would share to a high degree, if not completely. It is not clear what exactly this would include. It would obviously include the size and shape of my body, my hair and eye color, and perhaps some behavioral tendencies like my nervous twitches and my fondness for Belgian beer. Maybe it would include much more specific details of who I am. Nevertheless, I still do not think that this can be what we value in our personal existence, even if genetics determine one's behavior and personality to a very high degree.

Suppose, for example, that some mad scientist felt the need to kill me (perhaps because I "know too much"). He does not really want to kill me, however, and actually feels rather bad about it. So, to make it up to me, he decides that he will take a sample of my cells and make a clone of me after I die, thus ensuring that at least the expression of my genes will live on, even though I will be dead. If this was what I valued in my existence, then I should be greatly relieved that these genes would exist and continue to be expressed after I am killed. However, I would not be at all relieved, and I would be rather indifferent to whether or not this mad scientist was true to his word and made the clone of me after I was dead or forgot about it and never got around to doing it. Furthermore, I doubt that many abortion opponents would approve of an abortion on the condition that one was later to make a clone of the aborted fetus!

What I value in my existence is not mere existence per se, nor is it my genes or the expression thereof. A third thing that Glenn and I share is the one fetus that became me but could have become Glenn instead. We have the same origin in that particular fetus. But this is not relevant unless we grant that the fetus itself has some significant moral status, which would beg the question in favor of the antiabortion argument. This was, after all, the kind of question that was to be avoided by appeal to the golden rule approach. So we cannot appeal to it now to support the golden rule argument against abortion.

Fourth, there are the qualities and dispositions that make up one's character and personality. These are things that Glenn and I might share, depending on the extent to which genetic determinism is true or how similar our experiences are growing up. But who I take myself to be, how I think of who I am, is more than just a description of my beliefs, values, and dispositions. This is how other people think of me, especially those who do not know me intimately and who have not known me for a long time. How I think of myself, however, is largely through the particular life that I have lived. The best account of who I am is not a description of me but something more like the story of my life. If we want to know who Hitler was, or who Abe Lincoln was, a description or character sketch would not be very satisfying. A relatively complete biography (or perhaps even better, autobiography) would come closer to the essence of who these people were. Much, if not most, of what I see myself to be and value in my existence is based on the narrative of my experiences. Even my character, attitudes, and personality play a limited role in my personal sense of self; of crucial importance is how my character came to be developed, how I acquired my attitudes and personality traits, those life experiences that molded me into the person I am.

It does not seem to matter whether or not, or to what extent, Glenn resembles me from the outside, from a third-person perspective. We would still differ on the inside. All of the experiences of his life that constitute his own sense of self would be different from mine. Even if all of his life experiences were very similar, they would not be the same. We value our existence not for its own sake but for the things that happen to us in our lives, the things we do and experience. I do not value the existence of whomever the fetus that became me might have become but only the existence of that person who the fetus did become, namely me. I do not value equally all the lives that I might have lived. I have a special attachment to my own actual life, the one that I am in fact living.

In order to determine whether we could consent to having been raised by different parents, and thus having a different set of life experiences, we should imagine that a mad scientist (that's right, another mad scientist example!) had developed a way to erase and re-record thoughts in the human brain as if it were a videotape or compact disc. This scientist is intending to erase all your thoughts and memories and replace them with an entirely different set of thoughts and memories. You must ask yourself whether you could reasonably consent to having this done. I would not agree to undergo this procedure no matter how much I would be compensated after the erasure, because I would not consider the person with new memories to be me. I would consider this to be barely different from my being killed and an entirely new person created who would then inhabit what used to be my body. It would be little or no consolation to me that this new person would be similar to me and have similar thoughts, even many of the same beliefs, tastes, and personality traits.

The formal golden rule argument against abortion claims that approving of abortion commits you to consenting to the abortion of the fetus that was to become you and thus consenting to your own nonexistence. Since you would not consent to your own nonexistence, you cannot think that abortion is OK. However, approving of being raised by different parents, according to a similar use of the formal golden rule, commits you to consenting to having all of your experiences being different, as if the entire narrative of your life were erased and replaced by an entirely different set of experiences. Since you would probably not consent to that, you cannot think that adoption would be morally OK. (Or if you were adopted, then you cannot think it is morally OK for parents *not* to give their children up for adoption.) But that is an absurd conclusion, so the golden rule cannot meaningfully be applied to the existence of potential people.

On the other hand, the pro-lifer could try to save the golden rule argument against abortion by challenging the claim that Glenn and I are different people. Instead, one might say that Glenn is the same person as me but living a different life. If I had been raised by my biological family, I would be Glenn. Then one could say that although I prefer being the person who I am now, I would still prefer being a different person over not existing at all. I would rather be Glenn than not be anyone. However, it is very unclear what it means to say that "I would be a different person." If I say "I wish I were Paul," what I probably mean is that I wish I were in Paul's situation or that I had some of the things he has—his virtues, his high-paying job, or his hot girlfriend. It does not make sense for me to wish that I were him completely, because then (to put it crudely) it would not be *me*-being-him but *him*-being-him. A major part of what makes me the person that I take myself to be would not be the same had the fetus that became me grown up to become Glenn instead.

One might object that my inability to identify with Glenn does not mean that he is not the same person as me. It is very difficult for me to see myself as the same person now that I was twenty years ago, but that does not mean that I am not the same person as I was twenty years ago. In some sense this is certainly true. It is very difficult to imagine myself as I was then in that situation with the same interests, beliefs, and attitudes. But in another sense it is very easy to see myself as being the same as that person because I remember being that person. I remember what happened to him (me) and what he (I) did. And I remember this differently from how I remember what happens in other people's lives; I remember it *from the inside*. That person's experiences, actions, and beliefs make up a large part of my personal identity now and constitute part of the narrative of my life, no matter how different they might be from my current experiences, actions, and beliefs. We should, and most of us probably do, think of personal identity as temporally extended. This is why I can be ashamed of what I did twenty years ago, even if it is not something I would do now. I would not, however, feel any shame for anything that Glenn does.

Although it is true that I could not consent to being raised by my biological parents, I cannot infer that it would be wrong for me to have been raised by my birth mother because the argument would apply equally to Glenn. It would seem that I must judge it to have been wrong for my biological parents to raise me themselves while Glenn must judge it to be wrong for them to give him up for adoption. This, however, makes no sense—we are talking about the same parents deciding the fate of one and the same fetus. They cannot both keep *and* give him up.

FUTURE PEOPLE

At first glance it might seem that criticisms of the formal golden rule application to the fetus would also apply to application of the golden rule to future generations. If the indeterminacy of the identity of a potential person gave us reason to think that we have no moral obligation toward the person who the fetus might become, then it might also be reason to think that we have no obligations now to promote the interests of future generations since, at the present time, their identity is indeterminate. The pro-lifer would point out that this is absurd; obviously we do have obligations to future generations regardless of the indeterminacy of their particular identity. We have an obligation, for example, not to use up all of the earth's resources and not to render the earth uninhabitable for future people. If this line of reasoning is correct, then there must be some mistake in the rejection of the golden rule argument against abortion. We should be able to apply the golden rule to treatment of future people, so why not to the future person the fetus will become?

The problem with arguing that our duties to future generation also apply to the fetus is that it confuses potential or possible persons with future persons, and it confuses two kinds of obligations: (1) the obligation to allow a possible or potential person to become an actual future person and (2) the obligation to benefit, or not to harm, actual future persons. Future persons differ from merely potential persons in that future persons are not merely potential. They are *actual* persons who really will exist in the future, whereas a potential person might never become an actual person if it fails to develop or if it has an accident. Even if we accept the indeterminacy of potential people, we can still insist that it would be wrong to knowingly harm these actual future people, for example, by making the earth's environment inhospitable or by taking drugs during pregnancy that might cause birth defects. Though they may be only potential persons now, when the future persons suffer these harms in the future, they will be actual persons with determinate identities.

We can, however, deny that we have any obligation to ensure the *existence* of future persons. We might have an obligation not to harm them because, and insofar as, they will be actual persons. But if they are not allowed to come into existence, then they are not, and will never be, actual persons. In that case they cannot be harmed because they do not exist. It is not wrong to preclude the existence of particular potential persons. We have an obligation to future persons because they are persons, not because of who they are in particular. Likewise, it is not obvious that my biological mother had any obligation to make sure that this future person, me, existed rather than some other future person, or any future person at all.

This gives the pro-choicer a solution to a puzzle presented by the pro-life side. The pro-lifers argue that if it is wrong to harm a potential person, for example by taking a drug that will cause it to be born blind, then surely it is even more wrong to destroy a potential person (causing it to not be born at all). The distinction between potential persons and actually existing future persons, however, shows that it is not inconsistent to claim that abortion is morally acceptable but that it is morally wrong to intentionally cause birth defects in a fetus that one intends to carry full term and expects to develop normally. In the first case, one is merely denying existence to a future person (or to an indefinite number of different potential future persons who share the same genes), while in the second case one is causing a definite harm to some actual particular person in the future.

There is, however, one last pro-life argument. If the pro-choicer argues that the indeterminacy of future persons means that we cannot apply the golden rule to the fetus, then it also means that we cannot apply it to babies either (especially when one considers that it is not fetuses that are adopted but babies). This might imply that infanticide is morally acceptable. However, this objection is based on a misunderstanding of the pro-choice criticism of the golden rule argument against abortion. The consideration of the indeterminacy of potential persons is not any part of an argument *for* the moral permissibility of abortion; it does not support the positive claim that abortion is morally OK. It intends only to show that the golden rule cannot be applied to the abortion case because it relies on the particular identity of the person that the fetus will become, and this identity is indeterminate. This would mean that the formal golden rule also fails to show that infanticide is wrong. Thus the indeterminacy problem does not prove that abortion is not wrong, only that if it is wrong it must be wrong for some reason other than the golden rule. The same is true for infanticide.

SUGGESTED FURTHER READING

Boonin-Vail, David. "Against the Golden Rule Argument against Abortion." *Journal of Applied Philosophy* 14 (1997): 187–97.

Gensler, Harry. "A Kantian Argument against Abortion." *Philosophical Studies* 49 (1986): 83–98.

Hare, R. M. "A Kantian Approach to Abortion." *Social Theory and Practice* 15 (1989): 1–14.

———. "Abortion and the Golden Rule." *Philosophy and Public Affairs* 3 (1975): 201–22.

Meyers, Chris. "Abortion, Indeterminacy, and the Golden Rule Argument against Abortion." *Journal of Value Inquiry* 39 (2005): 459–73.

Wilson, Bryan. "On a Kantian Argument against Abortion." *Philosophical Studies* 53 (1988): 119–30.

CHAPTER 8

RIGHTS OF THE PREGNANT WOMAN

T hus far, the focus in this book has been on the moral status of the fetus, and up until this point we have largely neglected the rights of the pregnant woman and the moral significance, if any, of the relationship between the pregnant woman and her fetus. When we did consider the pregnant woman and her relation to the fetus, it was only in the accusatory terms of the "responsibility" argument. (And we found this argument, in all of its forms, to be rather weak.) There is a reason for this focus on the fetus and neglect of the pregnant woman: We have been primarily analyzing the arguments on the pro-life side, the arguments for the claim that abortion is morally wrong. Most of these arguments (at least most of the decent ones) tend to focus on the fetus and its alleged moral rights. Aside from the issues we addressed in chapter 5 (on responsibility), the pro-life arguments tend to neglect the interests and rights of the pregnant woman—apart from making exceptions for abortions that are necessary for her health or for terminating pregnancies that result from rape. So we have had no occasion to examine the pregnant woman's side of the issue. But that will all change once we consider one of the main arguments on the pro-choice side.

"IT'S MY BODY, I CAN ABORT IF I WANT TO"

The most common pro-choice argument appeals to the slogan "it is *the woman's* body." The principle that this slogan seems to invoke is that one should have the right to do whatever one wants with one's own body. Unfortunately, this principle is rarely formulated precisely or argued for explicitly in the public discourse.

On an extremely unfavorable reading we could apply this principle in absurd ways. For example, I might say that I have the right to swing my fists about wildly—never mind if one of them strikes an innocent person in the face. After all, it is *my* body; these are my fists and I can do what I want with them. This, however, is obviously not what is intended by the "my-body" principle. So first we need to more carefully formulate our principle and explain what it means so that we can prevent it from being twisted by those who want to play word games rather than engage in serious argument.

The most plausible formulation of the my-body principle is something like this: "All persons have a right to determine (insofar as they can) what happens in and to their own bodies, as long as by doing so they do not thereby infringe upon the rights of others." Those who accept this principle would also probably want to qualify it, especially by limiting "persons" to exclude young children, crazy people, and anyone else who is not capable of making competent choices. We would never, for example, allow a young child to undergo a sex-change operation or even to get a tattoo.

The my-body principle does not provide a very strong support for the pro-choice position, at least not without begging the question. The principle, properly qualified, would support only the pro-choice position given certain assumptions about the nature and moral status of the fetus, such as the assumption that the fetus cannot be harmed and has no moral rights. And these are assumptions that the pro-lifer would reject. If the fetus has rights that would be violated by the abortion, then our principle would not apply, for our principle states that a person can do whatever she wants with her own body *as long she does not thereby violate the rights of another*.

HAVEN'T WE ALREADY SHOWN THAT THE FETUS LACKS RIGHTS?

Now, it is true that we found most of the arguments on the pro-life side for fetal rights or for the special moral status of the fetus to be wanting. The substantive vitalism version of the soul, the future-like-ours, and the golden rule arguments have all failed to give us a definitive reason to think that we owe any moral obligations to the fetus. But to show that an argument for a certain conclusion fails is not enough to show that the conclusion is false.

The mistake we need to avoid making is what philosophers refer to as the "appeal to ignorance" fallacy. This faulty mode of reasoning basically works this way: "You have not proven X to be true, therefore X is false." For example, I could say "You cannot prove that there is life on other planets, therefore there is no life on other planets." The falsity of a claim surely does not follow from the mere lack of support for it. (And, alternatively, the truth of a claim does not follow from lack of proof against it.) We need to provide some positive reasons for thinking that something is true or false. At any rate, I am sure that the pro-choice side would not be satisfied with their position being affirmed merely as the default position. They would claim that there are better reasons for being pro-choice than merely a lack of evidence for the pro-life view.

One way to get around this problem is to show not only that all the arguments for the moral rights of the fetus fail, but to give positive reasons for thinking that the fetus has no moral rights and cannot be harmed. This is a very difficult task, because arguing, through logical reasoning alone, that the fetus has no moral status would require that we show that there is something absurd or contradictory in the idea that the fetus has some moral status. And even if we could present such an argument, it is not likely to convince anyone among the pro-life crowd or those who are ambivalent about abortion.

Another, better strategy that the pro-choice side could take, however, is to show that it *does not matter* whether or not the fetus has any special moral status. The claim would be that a woman has a right to terminate her pregnancy *even if the fetus has a right to life*. More generally, we would say that the woman has the right to determine what happens in, and to, her own body *even if* exercising that right will result in the death of the fetus. This would be a very powerful argument indeed, for it would mean that the pro-choice side could concede all or most of the claims that the pro-lifers usually make in support of their stance and yet still win the argument.

Compare this argumentative strategy with the following fact about the game of chess. For all the emphasis on careful positioning and winning the exchange, there is only one move that really matters in a chess game, and that is the move that checkmates the opponent. It does not matter if you fall behind in material or lose control of the center as long as you have the combination of moves that end in checkmate (for the other guy). It is similar with an argument. All that matters is the final move from the premises (the evidence) to the conclusion. If the pro-choicers could grant that a fetus has a right to life and yet still show that the woman has the right to an abortion, this would be analogous to sacrificing one's queen in order to checkmate the opposing king. You can give up on the battles and still win the war.

A CONFLICT OF RIGHTS

In 1971, philosopher Judith Thomson published a bold strategy in a now-famous article. It is one of the first major philosophy articles written on the abortion issue and is considered a classic. Just about every college student who has studied the abortion issue in a philosophy class has probably read this article. Let us consider Thomson's main argument, referred to as the "violinist argument" (for reasons that will soon be obvious), and then look at some of the criticism that might be given by philosophers as well as by nonphilosophers.

But before we examine the violinist argument, an important detail must be addressed. There is one assumption that is crucial to this violinist argument, and that is that a person has the right to decide what is allowed to happen in and to her own body. Each person, at least every rational, mature person, has the right to do what she wants with her own body *and* the right to forbid others from deciding what happens in and to her body without her consent.

There is not space in this book to argue for such a right, but I hope that it will be obvious and something we can all agree on, at least after we consider what it means and what kind of specific moral judgments it underwrites. For one, it is this right that makes it wrong (and illegal, at least in the United States) to perform surgery or other medical procedures on a person without her consent. It would be wrong (and illegal) to force a woman to have an abortion against her will, even if we thought that having an abortion was the best thing for her *and* for the fetus. This is why those who favor abortion rights call themselves "pro-choice." On their view, mandatory abortions would be at least as unjust as banning abortions, if not more so. Here is a more mundane example: No matter how badly Mr. Jones needs a triple bypass surgery, we cannot perform one on him if he refuses (assuming he is lucid and rational). On a more sinister note, it is also wrong to perform medical experiments on people without their informed consent. This right to the use of one's own body is also the right to be free from sexual coercion, even by one's spouse. To deny that people have a right to the use of their own body would be to imply that rape is acceptable and that it may be OK to use people as guinea pigs against their will.

So now let us propose that the fetus is a full person (not just a potential person) and that, accordingly, it has a full right to life—as much of a right to life as you or I have. Remember, we are granting this *for the sake of argument*. We are assuming it to be true in order to see if it really matters for the abortion question. The pro-choicer can grant the fetus a right to life for the sake of argument while still holding that the fetus does not have any such right.

If we accept that the woman has a right to determine the use of her own body, and we allow (for the sake of argument) that the fetus has a right to life, then what we seem to have is a conflict of rights held by two different parties. The pregnant woman's right to her own body conflicts with the fetus's right to life. It would be inevitable, in such a situation, that someone's rights are going to have to be violated, either the pregnant woman's or the fetus's (unless the issue resolves itself, such as with a spontaneous miscarriage). Either the woman is denied an abortion and is compelled to allow the fetus to use her body without her consent or the pregnancy is terminated and the fetus is denied its right to life.

In a situation where there is a conflict of rights we often judge that one right outweighs the other right. The following is an obvious example: In the United States, as well as most democratic and industrialized nations, we recognize a right to the freedom of religion. I have a right to believe whatever I want to about God and the divine (including that there is no God), and I can worship and practice my beliefs however I want—even if my religious views are seen as silly to others. I can practice Christianity, Islam, Zoroastrianism; I can even believe in the Flying Spaghetti Monster if I want to. No one may rightfully hinder me from doing so. But now suppose that I decide to convert to the ancient Aztec religion and try to practice my beliefs by making a human sacrifice to the god Huitzilopochtli. Now it seems that my right to practice my religious beliefs conflicts with another person's right to life (specifically, that of my intended sacrificee). Any reasonable person would say that the person's right to life outweighs my right to practice my religion, at least in this case.

It might seem intuitively obvious at first glance that the right to life should outweigh all other rights, since it is the most basic right. If so, then the fetus's right to life would automatically outweigh the pregnant woman's right to her own body—end of story. But this common assumption is exactly what Thomson denies, and her argument is intended to show why this seemingly commonsense judgment is mistaken.

THE VIOLINIST ARGUMENT

The pro-life argument assumes, as a basic principle, that the right to life (of the fetus) automatically outweighs the pregnant woman's right to the use of her own body. If that basic principle were true, then it should apply equally to cases other than abortion, in which one person's right to life conflicts with another person's right to her own body. So Thomson asks her reader to consider this hypothetical, and admittedly far-fetched, scenario. Imagine that you wake up in the morning and find yourself in a hospital bed with tubes surgically implanted into your back connecting you to some man you have never seen before. This man, it turns out, is a famous violinist who suffers from some rare and fatal kidney disease. (Thomson concocts the case this way because, as a rational, adult human being the man has as much of a right to life as anyone, and as a great violinist he also has substantial value to society.) For some reason, dialysis will not work on his condition and the only effective treatment is for him to be hooked up to a live human being. A society of music lovers searched through medical records, and your blood type was the closest match they could find to his. So they kidnapped you in the middle of the night, snuck you into the hospital, and had you hooked up to their beloved virtuoso. You protest to the doctor, who apologizes for the inconvenience and says what the music lovers did to you was wrong, but now that you are attached, you cannot be disconnected from the violinist because he would immediately die. The doctor tries to reassure you by saying that it will only be for nine months, and then the violinist will have recovered. There is only a small risk to your health, as well as considerable inconvenience. But, the doctor says, since the violinist's right to life outweighs your right to the use of your body, we cannot unhook you (and, in fact, we must prohibit you from detaching yourself).

Thomson assumes that her readers would agree that the doctor's position is outrageous. Of course, maybe you should stay hooked up to the violinist;

it would be a very nice thing for you to do. We might even say that it would be somewhat callous and selfish of you to unplug yourself from the violinist and allow him to die (though I don't think I would go that far). But certainly it is within your rights to unplug yourself from him, and it would be wrong for anyone to prevent you from unplugging yourself.

LIMITS TO WHAT THE VIOLINIST ARGUMENT SHOWS?

Now, some people will latch onto the idea that you were kidnapped. You did not volunteer to be this man's human dialysis machine. Thus they might be tempted to argue that the violinist case is analogous to getting pregnant as the result of being raped. So if that argument does show that abortion is permissible, it only shows that abortion should be allowed in cases of pregnancy resulting from rape. Many people who are otherwise against abortion want to make exception for these sorts of cases. On their view, women who consented to sex and got pregnant as a result should not be allowed to have an abortion, while women who were coerced into sex and got pregnant as a result should be allowed to end their pregnancy.

This position seems to have a lot of intuitive appeal, considering the large number of people who accept the relevance of rape as a factor for determining when abortion is acceptable. But does this position hold up? If we should not allow women generally to have an abortion, then why should we make an exception for rape victims? One of the reasons why some people accept the relevancy of rape is because they accept some version of the responsibility argument. Abortion, or perhaps having an unwanted pregnancy, is seen as irresponsible (or having sex is seen as "dirty"). If the woman got pregnant as the result of rape, then she was not being irresponsible. But we have already rejected these sorts of arguments back in chapter 5.

Another reason why someone might accept the relevancy of rape as a legitimate exception could be the claim that by consenting to sex the woman has consented to having the fetus use her womb, or even that she has thereby made an implicit promise to the fetus that she will carry it to term. This, however, seems flawed on several counts. For one, by agreeing to have sex, the woman has made an agreement only with her sexual partner, not with any third parties. Also, it does not seem to make sense to say that the woman has made a promise, implicit or otherwise, to the fetus, since the fetus did not yet exist at the time of the sexual encounter. Furthermore, what if the woman used contraception and it failed? It seems that the use of contraception, insofar as it is an attempt to prevent the fetus from being conceived, implies that the woman did not invite the fetus into her womb and so there is no promise to care for it.

Most important, Thomson argues that the kidnapping is irrelevant to the pro-life argument under consideration. This argument is based on the principle that one person's right to life outweighs another person's right to decide what happens in and to her own body. How the person came to be—or came to be attached to you—is irrelevant to whether he has a right to life. Now if it were the violinist himself who had kidnapped you, then we might be able to say that he has forfeited his rights and so may rightfully be disconnected. But we are assuming that the violinist is innocent and had no hand in the music lovers' plan to abduct you. (Maybe we can just assume that the violinist is unconscious through all this.)

If this is not convincing, then we can simply change the case slightly. Suppose that you are at least partly responsible for the situation of being hooked up to the violinist. Suppose it is partly the result of your own carelessness. Let us say that this is not the first time that this has happened. This society of music lovers has kidnapped people in the past, creating quite a controversy that made newspaper headlines and was all over the TV news. Suppose you heard about a sick violinist, and you had reason to suspect that you might be a close match to his blood type (perhaps you and he share a very similar ethnic background). Now suppose you accept an invitation to have tea at the society of music lovers, during which they drug the tea and hook you up to the violinist. Certainly your actions were imprudent, perhaps even foolish or reckless—just as it would be imprudent to have sex without contraception if one does not want to get pregnant. But that does not mean that you no longer have the right to determine what happens to your own body. And similarly, having sex—even knowing that it might result in pregnancy—also does not mean that you no longer have the right to determine what happens to your own body.

What if you volunteered to be a human dialysis for the violinist but then changed your mind? You cannot sign away the right to your own body any more than you can sign away your freedom by selling yourself into slavery, or sign away your right to life by making a suicide pact. If a woman changes her mind and decides, during foreplay, that she does not want to engage in sexual intercourse, that is her right and it would still be rape for someone to force her, no matter how willing she might have been up to that point.

To use a better analogy, suppose I invited a stranger into my house on a cold day to warm himself. After a few hours, I find him to be very annoying, and he smells bad. I ask him to leave and he refuses. When the police show up, is there nothing they can do? Since I invited him, did I relinquish the right to decide what happens in my own house? Now suppose that it is freezing outside and that this stranger might not survive. Can I not still kick him out of my house? It might be callous and cruel, but to say that I have no right to make him leave is to deny that I have a right to do what I want with my own property. Because I invited him in, my house must now become a homeless shelter.

A DUTY TO ALLOW ABORTIONS

The violinist argument is not intended to show that abortion is morally OK but rather that it would be morally wrong to prevent a woman from terminating her pregnancy if she wanted to. It would be morally wrong to compel a woman to carry a fetus in her womb and to give birth to it against her will. The argument leaves open whether or not having an abortion itself is morally wrong. In other words, abortion should be allowed, even if we should morally disapprove of it.

It might sound odd at first to say that there are things we have reason to morally disapprove of and yet should allow people to do—that we should even defend their right to act in morally wrong ways. But the question of whether the woman herself should have an abortion is a very different question from whether we should try to stop her. There are many instances where it would be wrong to compel people to act in morally acceptable ways. We might, for example, disapprove of people who are lazy (and it might be correct for us to disapprove of them). But that does not make it morally OK for us to compel such people to work. I am not saying that we need to support those who can work and choose not to; but if someone can afford to provide for himself without being a burden to anyone else and chooses to lie around watching soap operas while letting his talents go to waste, that is his right even if we think it is wrong for him to do so. Forcing him to work against his will is tantamount to slavery. This is simply a matter of what it means to have a "right." To have a right to X (freedom of speech, control over your own body, etc.) simply means that others must allow you to enjoy or practice X, and that others must be prohibited from denying you X.

All this is not to say that abortion is morally wrong or that we should disapprove of it. The point is that *even if* it is morally wrong, it is nevertheless the woman's right to do it, and so it would be morally wrong to try to prevent her from doing so (and others have a duty to prohibit you from preventing her). Some people might think that you have a moral obligation to help the violinist and let him use your body, while some might say that you have no such obligation and that there would be nothing wrong with unplugging yourself and walking away. The point is that, since he has no right to your body, we cannot *compel* you to let him use it even if you ought to let him. Even if it is selfish to deny him your help, you have the right to be selfish when it comes to your own body, and no one can rightfully force you to let another use it without your consent.

POSITIVE VERSUS NEGATIVE RIGHTS

Why should we agree that the woman's right to her own body should outweigh the fetus's right to life? After all, certainly the right to life is much more weighty and important than the right to one's own body. If we had to choose to give up one rather than the other, I think that virtually all rational people would hold onto their right to life and choose to part with the right to determine what happens to their own body. This is partly due to the fact that the right to determine what happens in and to your own body is of very little value without the right to life. If I were to be killed, I would find very little consolation in the fact that others would not be allowed to violate my corpse.

Most people cherish life more than freedom and autonomy (at least with regard to their body), and this is reasonable since the one is a necessary condition for the other. For this reason, philosophers have argued that the right to life is a more basic or fundamental right. For a right to be more basic than another right means that it has a logical priority over the less basic right. The more basic rights are necessary for the less basic rights to be meaningful.

Does this mean that one person's more basic right should outweigh another person's less basic right? Should the violinist's right to life (being more basic) take priority over your right to the use of your own body (being less basic)? Before we answer this question we must take a closer look into the nature of moral rights in general, and more specifically into what it means to say that someone has a right to her own body and what it means to say that someone has a right to life.

A right is a complex concept, and rights can be divided into different types along many dimensions. There is one distinction, however, that is especially crucial to our question of whether the right to life should override the right to one's own body—that is the distinction between "positive" rights and "negative" rights. This is an essential distinction that cuts across all other categories of rights.

A *negative* right is an absolute protection from the interference of others. It is a right to be left alone in some particular way, to be free from certain kinds of harm or coercion. It consists of the liberty to engage in certain activities without being prevented from (or punished for) doing so. A negative right obligates all others to refrain from trying to deny you those things that you have a right to (and this obligation can be compelled). They are called "negative" rights because they obligate others *not* to do certain things. Thus, having a right to freedom of speech means that others must not censure you or try to silence you or punish you for speaking your mind. (Of course, there are limits; a right to freedom of speech does not allow for one to incite a riot or commit slander.) A right to your property means that others must not take from you what is rightfully yours without your permission. Even the right to a fair trial is a negative right, for what it really means is that others may *not* punish you without first proving you to be guilty through an impartial trial. To have a negative right means that others have negative duties toward you, duties *not* to do certain things. And as a right, others can be compelled to meet these negative duties.

To have a *positive* right, on the other hand, is to be entitled to certain goods or services. Positive rights obligate others not merely to stand idly by and leave you alone but to provide you with some kind of assistance. A positive right gives other people positive duties, duties to act in some way, not merely duties to refrain from acting. Most of the rights we commonly think of are negative rights. Such rights do not compel others to help; they merely dictate that others stay out of the way and do no harm. The right to freedom of speech, for example, means that I must not try to prohibit you from speaking your mind, but I do not need to help you express yourself by providing you with a forum or distributing pamphlets preaching your crazy ideas. It is up to you to spread your own message. Your right to freedom of religion means that I cannot try to prevent you from practicing your religion. But I have no obligation to help you practice your religion by building you a church and stocking it with clergy. It is up to you to provide your own means to worship.

Examples of alleged positive rights might include the right to a certain degree of education or the right to adequate healthcare. The right to an education is positive, not negative, because to have such a right would mean that others are obligated not merely to allow you to obtain an education but to provide for schools and staff them with teachers. A right to healthcare would be a positive right because it means not only that others shall not prohibit you from obtaining medical treatment but that when you get to the hospital the doctor is obligated to treat you (if you are sick or injured).

Because a positive right is a right, these positive duties can be compelled. Not only should others try to help you in these ways, but they can justly be forced to help you. This leads to a problem for positive rights. Who exactly is it who is obligated to provide these entitlements guaranteed by positive rights? Surely the right to healthcare cannot obligate *me* to provide others with adequate healthcare, for I have no medical skills and lack the means to pay other people's medical bills. This is not a problem for negative rights. Who exactly is it that my right to free speech obligates? The answer is everyone. Everyone must refrain from trying to silence me or punish me for speaking my mind.

Another problem with positive rights is that it may not be possible to fulfill them, at least not completely. We might not, for instance, have the resources to provide every human being in the world with adequate healthcare. If it is not possible to provide it, then we cannot be obligated to provide it. (We cannot be morally obligated to do that which is impossible.) If we are not obligated to provide it, then they cannot have a right to it. This is not to say that we have no moral duty to provide as much as we can. But if we cannot provide it to everyone, then we do not violate the rights of those we were unable to help. Again, this is not a problem for negative rights. We can respect everyone's right to freedom of speech, for example, by never interfering with anyone who is peacefully expressing her views.

For these and other reasons, negative rights generally have priority over positive rights. Some philosophers would even go so far as to deny that there are any positive rights at all. Again, denying that there are positive rights does not mean that there are no positive duties, just that those on the receiving end of such actions are not entitled to our help. Though we should help them if we can, we cannot legitimately be forced to help. Of course, some philosophers deny that there are any moral rights, positive or negative. They prefer instead to employ different moral concepts, but this need not concern us here. We will assume, for the sake of argument, that there are moral rights, including the right to life and the right to the use of one's own body.

POSITIVE VERSUS NEGATIVE RIGHT TO LIFE

Having made, and I hope clarified, the important distinction between positive and negative rights, we must decide in which category the right to life belongs. If we interpret the right to life as a merely negative right, then it means a right not to be killed. It would be a protection from having your life taken away and would obligate others to *allow* you to continue to live. And as a right, others can be compelled, by force if necessary, to refrain from killing you. If, on the other hand, we interpret the right to life as a positive right, then it would mean that you are entitled to be provided with everything you need to survive. It would obligate others to do whatever is necessary to help you continue living. And as a right, others could be compelled, by force if necessary, to provide such help.

We should interpret the right to life as merely a negative right, the right not to be killed. This is not to say that we have no moral obligation to help others survive or to try to provide the means that others require in order to continue living. It is only to say that we cannot compel others to meet these obligations, especially if it requires significant risk or sacrifice on their part. Perhaps I have a moral duty to run into a burning building and save those people inside who might be unconscious due to smoke inhalation. Perhaps you might morally disapprove of me if I don't, calling me selfish or cowardly. But those inside do not have a *right* to my assistance. It would be wrong for others to force me into the building, at significant risk to myself, for the benefit of those who might still be inside.

TERMINATING THE PREGNANCY VERSUS KILLING THE FETUS

What all of this means is that the woman has the right to deny the fetus the use of her body, just as you would have the right to unplug yourself from the violinist. And this right is not outweighed by the fetus's (or the violinist's) right to life because that right is only the right not to be killed and does not entitle the fetus (or the violinist) to be provided with the means to survive.

But this is problematic. It seems obvious that ending the pregnancy (having an abortion) is the same thing as killing the fetus. Let us compare this to unplugging the violinist. You know the violinist is going to die if he is unplugged from you, so aren't you killing him by unplugging him? Maybe, maybe not. This may largely be a semantic issue. The important thing is to consider what it is that you have a right to. You have a right to determine the use of your own body (including denying others from using it, even if that means the violinist dies). You do not have the right to the violinist being dead. If, by some miracle, he were to survive after you unplugged yourself from him, you cannot then turn around and slash his throat. Likewise, according to the violinist argument, the pregnant woman has the right to deny the fetus the use of her body, even if that means that the fetus dies. But she cannot rightfully strangle the baby after she has given birth to it. For this reason, Thomson's violinist argument only allows for abortion before the fetus is viable outside of the womb.

The pro-lifer would likely protest at this point, and reasonably so. Abortion does not simply involve "unplugging" a fetus. The fetus is not removed intact from the uterus, and its death is not the result of being detached from the pregnant woman's womb. Rather, the fetus is destroyed in the process of being removed. (Abortion procedures differ, but most of them involve destroying or dismantling the fetus as it is removed.) These are the unpleasant facts about abortion. But does it really matter exactly how the fetus is removed, or what the actual cause of death is? It is true that the fetus is killed in an abortion; it does not just die on its own. Nevertheless, it is killed in the act of removing it. It is not killed *after* it is removed. The fetus is only killed in the abortion because (1) it must be dismembered in order to remove it safely, and (2) it would not survive even if it were to be removed intact. Since the early fetus is incapable of feeling pain, it does not seem to matter exactly how it dies.

Let us go back to the violinist example, to see whether the fact that the fetus is killed in the abortion really makes a difference. We have been assuming, I think, that what connects you to the violinist is an apparatus that could be unplugged from you (and/or him). But now imagine that the apparatus connecting your vital organs to his are surgically implanted into both your organs and his organs. If you render the connection asunder, then both of you will likely bleed to death. Instead the only way to disconnect yourself from him is to take the connecting pieces with you, along with some of his organs that the device is hooked up to. So, by disconnecting yourself from him, you tear out his vital organs and he dies as a result of your disconnecting him and not from the disease that required him to be hooked up to you (although he would have died of his disease shortly after being disconnected anyway). This difference regarding the specific cause of death by itself does not seem particularly significant. You unplug him and as a result he dies. It does not really matter if it was due to the unplugging itself or due to the disease that required him to be plugged in. If you have a right to unplug yourself (even if his life depends on being plugged into you), then it would be wrong for others to prevent you from unhooking him.

A MORE REALISTIC EXAMPLE

In the many years that I have taught philosophy, no reading assignment has inspired more groaning and complaining from my students than Thomson's abortion article and her violinist argument. Students complain that the example is ridiculously unrealistic; it would never happen. There is no real disease that requires such an unusual treatment, and no such device allowing people to be connected in that way. There are no such bands of music lovers so fanatically devoted to a musician that they would kidnap innocent people in this way, and no doctor would perform such a procedure on an unwilling patient (and no hospital would allow such a procedure to take place). I find the utter lack of imagination in my students, and their complete unwillingness to ponder somewhat fantastic scenarios, quite disappointing. Maybe television is to blame. Then again, if TV audiences can accept the bizarre scenarios of shows like *Lost* and the *X-Files*, why can't they accept the violinist case, at least as a hypothetical possibility?

Of course the violinist case is wildly implausible. There is no such illness, no such procedure, and no such band of music fascists in the real world. But none of that should matter. The violinist case is not to be considered for its own sake. Its purpose is to test the acceptability of the claim that one person's right to life outweighs another person's right to the use of her own body. If we accept such a principle, then it must apply to *all* cases, real and imaginary. Of course, the imaginary cases have to be possible cases, and they must be possible in our actual world (or one very similar to it). We cannot meaningfully test our principles in imaginary worlds where people live forever or are impervious to pain. Our moral principles must be partly grounded in facts about human nature and the human condition. But the violinist situation could possibly happen in our actual world—a world where people get sick and die, where people value their personal freedom, and so on.

If the principle that we are testing (that the right to life outweighs another's right to her body) does not work in the violinist case, then it should be rejected. Never mind that such a case has never occurred and probably never will occur. We must make similar moral judgments about similar situations, unless there is some morally relevant difference. If the violinist's right to life does not override your right to your own body, then neither does the fetus's right to life outweigh the pregnant woman's right to her body (unless there is some morally significant difference). The fact that one scenario is likely and the other one is unlikely is not a morally relevant difference.

Be that as it may, for those people who lack imagination or are too stubborn to suspend disbelief and apply a principle to a far-fetched case, let me present a more realistic situation. Suppose that, instead of some imaginary illness, the musician was suffering from ordinary kidney failure, and you are the only healthy person who is an exact match for his very rare blood type. If we grant that people have a right to life in the positive sense of being entitled to everything that they need to live, then the violinist is entitled to one of your kidneys. If this positive right outweighs your right to the use of your own body, then it would be morally OK for us to take one of your kidneys and donate it to the dying violinist. We need not imagine roaming hordes of music fanatics or unscrupulous doctors. We need only imagine a law to be passed allowing the harvesting of organs from unwilling "donors." (Maybe this law would not be passed in the United States today, but surely it is not unlikely that some country at some time could pass such a law.) Would it be morally OK for others to seize you and force you to undergo the surgery to remove one of your kidneys for the benefit of the sick violinist? Would you support this law? If your answer is no, then you do not think that one person's right to life should outweigh another's right to decide what happens to and in her own body.

Thomson probably chose her example because the violinist is already hooked up to the unwilling patient in the same way that, when abortion is being considered, the fetus has already staked out a place in the woman's uterus. The pro-lifer could insist that a right not to have your kidney taken thus only proves a right to avoid pregnancy, not a right to end a pregnancy that has already begun. But suppose that the doctors have already taken your kidney without your consent to save the violinist. (Perhaps you were under anesthesia to get your appendix removed.) Shouldn't you be able to sue the doctors and make them put your kidney back where it belongs (even though the violinist will die without it)?

THE RIGHT TO ONE'S PARENTS' BODIES?

The pro-lifer might object that there is an important difference between taking your kidney to save the violinist and forcing the pregnant woman to carry and give birth to the fetus, and that difference is that the violinist is a stranger to you, while the fetus is the pregnant woman's child. The violinist example (and the kidney example) is not an argument from analogy but rather a counterexample to the pro-life principle that another person's right to life outweighs your right to your own body. Of course, the pro-lifer can simply modify the principle to say that a child's right to life automatically outweighs a parent's right to her own body (but not a stranger's right to the use of her body). That the fetus is the pregnant woman's child and the violinist is a stranger would then be a morally relevant different between the two cases. The pro-choice crowd might insist that this qualification of the principle is ad hoc. But it is no matter. They can simply modify our example to accommodate the pro-lifer's modified principle. Instead of forcing some random stranger to donate his kidney to the violinist, we are going to take the kidney from the violinist's father.

Suppose our unfortunate violinist is told by his doctor that he needs a kidney transplant to live. The violinist's father is the only suitable donor. So the violinist asks his father for a kidney and his father turns him down, denying him the kidney even though he needs it to live. Before we judge the violinist's father too harshly we should note that there may be many reasons for his refusal to give up one of his own kidneys—just as there may be many reasons a woman might have for wanting to end a pregnancy. Some of these reasons will be good and some bad. Maybe the violinist has been a lousy son, neglecting his lonely parents and letting them languish in squalor while he lives it up in his mansion. Maybe the violinist's parents got divorced when he was very young and the father never got to know his son. There may be other reasons. Maybe the violinist has a host of other medical conditions and will probably not live more than a couple of months even with a healthy kidney. The father does not see why he should shorten his life by many years just so that his son can live an extra couple of weeks. Maybe the father has a serious medical condition and has very little chance of surviving with only one kidney. Maybe the father is a Jehovah's Witness or a member of the Christian Science church and believes that such medical procedures are forbidden by his religion. Maybe the father's reasons are much weaker. Maybe he simply does not want to have to carefully watch what he eats and drinks.

We may agree with some of these reasons, some we may think are deplorable, and others we may be ambivalent or uncertain about. The first thing we must keep in mind, however, is that we cannot say for certain what we would do if asked to donate a kidney. It is very easy to *say*, "I would not hesitate to donate one of my kidneys to a loved one!" Unless you have actually donated a kidney, or made some comparable sacrifice for someone else, then you cannot know for certain whether you would have the courage to go through with it. All I can say is that I *hope* I would be able to donate one of my kidneys (although what I really hope is that I will never be asked). That being said, I can still disapprove of the father's decision as long as I would be equally disapproving of my own decision if I did the same thing in the same situation.

Most of us will probably judge the father's refusal of his kidney to his son depending on his reasons. Maybe we should think the same way with abortion. There are good and bad reasons for terminating a pregnancy. Only the most callous fanatic would disapprove of a woman who terminated a pregnancy that threatened her life or health. It is also hard for anyone with a degree of sympathy to disapprove of aborting a fetus that will die anyway, such as a fetus with Tay-Sachs disease (100 percent fatal in the first few years of life) or anencephaly (no brain). On the other hand, even the most militant pro-choicers are appalled by those who would have an abortion just to avoid postponing a vacation.

When it is an issue of someone's moral right, however, the reasons and motives of those exercising their rights are irrelevant. The freedom of speech gives me the right to express my views even if they are unpopular. My reasons can be admirable, such as a desire to speak out against what I see as a grave injustice. Or my motives might be less noble. I might be trying to increase sales of a book I wrote or simply trying to antagonize those with opposing political views. My right to express myself does not depend on my reasons or motivation. To have a right to do something does not mean that it is morally right to do it. Sometimes exercising your right is morally objectionable. To have a right simply means that it would be wrong for others to prohibit you from exercising that right.

So maybe we think it might be morally wrong for the father not to donate his kidney to his son, and that will depend on his reasons. But whatever his reasons, it would be wrong for us to compel him to give up his kidney against his will. And if his kidney is taken without his consent, he should be able to demand that his kidney be restored to him. Ultimately only he can decide if his reasons for keeping his kidney are good enough. It is not up to us to decide, since it is, after all, *his* kidney. He may have a moral obligation to donate his kidney, but this is something we cannot force him to do since, if we take his kidney against his will, he would not be donating it. To "donate" means to give it freely. We cannot donate what is not ours, and so we cannot donate someone else's kidney.

The same, it seems, should be said about abortion. (And this, ultimately, is Thomson's thesis.) We may think that the woman who has an abortion and thereby denies the fetus the use of her body is selfish or callous—though that will probably depend on her reasons—but we still cannot and must not prevent her from exercising her right by forcing her to carry the fetus full term.

FROZEN EMBRYOS

The idea of taking someone's kidney against his will because another person needs it may seem far-fetched and unrelated to the issue of abortion. But the pro-life claim that the fetus has a positive right to life, and that this right can outweigh a person's (negative) right to bodily integrity, can have strange implications for the case of frozen embryos.

Frozen embryos are an inevitable by-product of in vitro fertilization. The process begins by harvesting eggs from the woman's ovaries. Because the harvesting of eggs is invasive, several eggs are obtained at once (so that it will not have to be done again in a month). Each egg is then fertilized in a petri dish with sperm from a male donor. The resulting zygote is then allowed to develop and multiply up to a certain point. The healthiest-looking embryo is then implanted into the uterus. The others are frozen, in case they are needed later. If all goes well, the embryo will implant into her uterine wall and, *voilà*, she will be pregnant. Unfortunately, as many as half of all conceptions (whether through ordinary sex or in vitro fertilization) fail to implant. If that is the case, then another embryo is selected, thawed, and injected into the uterus.

When pregnancy finally results, there are usually several embryos left-over in the freezer. What should be done with these? One possibility is to use them in medical research and eventually medical therapy. This research requires destroying the embryo. Embryos are made of stem cells, which promise miraculous treatments for a variety of ailments and injuries—especially ones involving damage to the nervous system. This is because the human body cannot grow new neurons, while stem cells can develop into any sort of human cell.

If embryos have a right to life (in the negative sense), then it would be wrong to destroy them—whether they are discarded *or* used for stem cells. Some women are willing to "adopt" these leftover embryos and have them implanted in their own wombs. But this should require the consent of the biological parents. The alternative is to leave them in the freezer indefinitely, where they will eventually deteriorate. If the embryo has a positive right to life, a right to have everything it needs to survive, then each should be given a chance for life. They should each be implanted into some woman's uterus—never mind if the biological parents object or if there are no willing volunteers to donate their wombs. Positive rights justify others to be compelled to provide what is needed. Thus, if the fetus has a positive right to develop and be born, then we can conscript fertile women for the use of their wombs. If you think this scenario sounds crazy, then you will agree that the fetus has no positive right to life.

DOUBTS ABOUT MORAL RIGHTS

The violinist argument has one key weakness, and that is that it assumes that each person has a moral right to the use of her own body. It is not so much this right in particular that is dubious, for any reasonable person would agree that we have a moral duty to respect other people's bodily integrity. What is dubious is the idea of moral rights.

The problem with moral rights is that, under the standard interpretation, they are *absolute* protections or entitlements. Moral rights are thought to outweigh all other moral considerations. Thus it would be wrong to violate someone's rights no matter how much good could be accomplished by doing so. This seems intuitively plausible if we consider carefully selected examples. Suppose there is a hospital where five patients are dying of organ failure. One needs a heart, one needs a liver, and so on. Unfortunately, there are no available organs, so all five will soon perish. Now an ambulance arrives and drops off an unconscious homeless man. This man got hit on the head and has a mild concussion. Once he awakens, we can give him a couple of aspirin and send him on his way. It just so happens, however, that his blood type is a perfect match for all five dying patients. (I guess it is a very small town.) The doctors realize that they could harvest this man's organs and save all five people. Though our poor homeless man would die, the five others would be saved. (Since he is homeless, presumably nobody would take much notice that he is no longer around.) It seems obvious to most people (at least in Western societies) that taking his organs against his will would be seriously wrong. This intuition supports a right to bodily integrity. Even if we took only nonvital organs—his gall bladder, one kidney, part of his liver—it still seems wrong. Taking nonvital organs would not violate his right to life, but it would violate his right to bodily integrity.

If we look at a different example, however, our intuitions will not support an absolute right to bodily integrity. Suppose doctors diagnose a man with cancer, but then, without any treatment, the man's tumor mysteriously disappears. Further experiments reveal that he has a unique ability to reverse cancerous tumors. With just a small sample of his DNA, scientists could replicate the genes responsible and cure cancer, saving countless people. Doctors ask the man for a DNA sample, which would require only a pinprick, and he refuses. They offer him rich incentives, including a substantial cut of the profits from the medicine. He still refuses. Would it be wrong for the doctors to take a DNA sample without his consent (even if they paid him the money they originally offered)? If he has an absolute right to bodily integrity, then it would be wrong, even though doing so would save hundreds of thousands of lives.

For these and other reasons, many philosophers reject the notion of absolute rights. (Jeremy Bentham referred to rights as "nonsense on stilts." And speaking of bodily integrity, incidentally, he had his body mummified and put on display at the University of London!) I myself have my doubts, at least about the *absolute* aspect. There are other ways that philosophers analyze moral issues without positing moral rights. One very popular way is to look at the consequences that result from actions or policies to determine their rightness (or wrongness). We will take that approach in the next chapter.

SUGGESTED FURTHER READING

Boonin-Vail, David. "Death Comes for the Violinist: On Two Objections to Thomson's 'Defense of Abortion.'" *Social Theory and Practice* 23 (1997): 329–64.

Silverstein, Harry. "On a Woman's *'Responsibility'* for the Fetus." *Social Theory and Practice* 13 (1987): 103–19.

Thomson, Judith Jarvis. "A Defense of Abortion." *Philosophy and Public Affairs* 2 (1973): 146–59.

Wilcox, John. "Nature as Demonic in Thomson's Defense of Abortion." *New Scholasticism* 63 (1989): 463–84.

CHAPTER 9

CONSEQUENCES

Many people appeal to moral rights when debating the abortion issue. But both sides can appeal to rights. Pro-lifers often claim that the fetus has a right to life, while the pro-choicer can claim that the woman has a right to choose. If rights are absolute, then no right can override (or be overridden by) any other right. As we saw in the previous chapter, however, the right to life is only a negative right, which does not obligate the pregnant woman to carry the fetus to term. The problem with that line of reasoning is that an abortion seems to do more than just remove the unwelcome fetus from the woman's uterus. For this reason, maybe we should avoid altogether any appeals to absolute rights.

Perhaps a better approach to tricky moral problems like this one is to look at the consequences of relevant actions or policies. What are the consequences of abortions or abortion policies? Would the world be a better place overall if we banned all abortions? Or would allowing abortions lead to better overall results? People on both sides of the abortion controversy appeal to good and bad consequences in their arguments. Some pro-lifers, for example, claim that abortion is "bad for women" in that it involves unnecessary health risks and often results in mental health problems. Many on the pro-choice side argue that a ban on abortion will lead to more unsafe, "back-alley" abortions. Before considering these specific arguments, however, we must first look at this general method of basing the moral rightness and wrongness of an action on its consequences.

UTILITARIANISM

There is a theory, popular among academic philosophers, that the rightness or wrongness of an action is determined entirely by the consequences. It is also a commonsense view reflected in such folk sayings as "All's well that ends well," or the somewhat darker proverb "The ends justify the means." This philosophical theory is known as *utilitarianism*. According to utilitarianism, the morally right action is the one that results in the best overall consequences. By "overall" we mean the consequences for everyone affected by the action (not just the person doing it), and we mean not only the immediate consequences but the long-term and indirect consequences as well.

Note that the morally right action is not just any act that has good consequences; it must have the *best* consequences. An act can have overall good consequences and still be wrong if there were another action one could have done that would have resulted in even better consequences. It is even possible, on this view, for a morally right action to have overall bad consequences. This would be the case if every course of action available would lead to a bad outcome—in other words, you are "damned if you do, damned if you don't." The right thing to do in that situation is to perform the act that would have the *least bad* consequences. After all, least bad is still the best.

Let us look at a particular example. Suppose that a friend of mine prepares an elaborate dinner for me. Unfortunately, despite her best efforts, the food is not very good (though it is still edible). I eat out of politeness, with the help of several glasses of wine, trying to forget the disappointing meal and instead focus on the enjoyable conversation. Halfway through our main course, however, she asks me, with hopeful anticipation, how I like the food. I know that she put forth great effort and would be crestfallen to hear the truth, no matter how tactfully I couch it. On the other hand, if I lie and say that the food is very good, she might cook for me again, and I will have to endure yet another unpalatable meal. Not to mention that if she discovers the lie, she will be even more upset than if I insulted her cooking. Either way it turns out badly, but probably less so if I tell the truth now.

It does not matter, according to the utilitarian theory, what *kind* of action it is. All that matters are the consequences. In some cases, lying might be the morally right thing to do, as long as it would have better consequences than telling the truth or saying nothing. This is not as counterintuitive as it might first seem. To use a philosophical cliché, imagine that you are living in Nazi Germany and you have Jewish friends hiding in your attic. The gestapo comes to your door and asks if there are any Jews in the household. Does anyone doubt that you should lie in order to protect the innocent? It is the morally right thing to do because lying will save lives and anything less than lying (confessing or saying nothing) will result in disastrous consequences for your unfortunate friends. The same could be said for stealing, breaking promises, even killing an innocent person. If such an action would have the best consequences, then it would be the morally right thing to do.

Of course, these situations are going to be very rare. Usually lying, stealing, and killing have much worse consequences than the alternatives. This is especially so when we consider the long-term and indirect consequences. Lying to my friend about her cooking might make her happy now but could cause trouble down the road. The fact that lying, stealing, and killing *usually* have such bad consequences explains why there is such a strong moral presumption against them. But the utilitarian would claim that it is superstition to thereby think that such actions are *always* wrong, regardless of the circumstances.

According to utilitarianism, right and wrong are not only independent of the kind of action; it also does not matter *why* you do it. All that matters is outcome, not motives. For example, I am taking a stroll on the beach when I see a child drowning in the water. There is no one else nearby, so I swim out and save the little bugger. Obviously this has better consequences than letting him drown; he gets to live the rest of life, and his family is spared the agony of losing a child. What if I saved him only in hopes of getting a reward? Maybe I thought his parents might be wealthy and would buy me a boat out of gratitude. Or I hoped to get my picture in the paper—"Local Philosopher Saves Boy"—and all the girls would think I am a hero. No matter how selfish my motives were, I still did the right action. Maybe another person, in the same situation, would have saved the child out of love of humanity or out of a desire to bring about the best overall consequences. This other guy might be a better person than me, but his act of saving the child is no more morally right than mine was. We both saved the kid and spared his family a lot of suffering. Utilitarianism is only a theory about what makes actions right or wrong, not a theory about what makes a person good or bad.

INTRINSICALLY GOOD (BAD)

In order to know which actions have the best consequences we need to figure out what sorts of things are good and what sorts are bad (and what sorts of things are neither good nor bad). Every action will have many consequences, some good, some bad, and some indifferent. Saving the drowning child will prevent his parents from mourning his death (good for them), it will get my clothes wet (bad for me), and it will create a wake in the water as I swim (indifferent, neither good nor bad).

There are two ways that things can be good or bad: they can be instrumentally good or bad, or they can be intrinsically good or bad. For something to be *instrumentally* good means that it leads to something else that is good. Money, for example, is not good in itself, but it can lead to other things that are good, such as pleasure or peace of mind. Likewise, instrumentally bad things lead to other things that are bad. For example, as I write this I am suffering from a bout of the chicken pox. The viral infection is not bad in itself. There is nothing bad about the fact that there happens to be vericella-zoster viruses in my body. Anyone who has ever had chicken pox still has the virus in her body, and that is not itself a bad thing. What is intrinsically bad is the suffering that the disease is now causing me. The chills I feel at night and the pain caused by the blisters all over my body are intrinsically bad. If the infection had no symptoms, then it would not be bad (nor good). Of course, some things can be both instrumentally good and instrumentally bad. Cigarette smoking causes pleasure in the short run (at least for regular smokers) and causes great suffering and shortened life span in the long run.

Something that is *intrinsically* good, on the other hand, is good in itself, good independently of how it came to be or what might follow. (Likewise, something that is intrinsically bad is bad in itself.) The list of things that might reasonably be called intrinsically good or bad is quite small. Most of the things we think of as good are only instrumentally good. Take good food, as an example (or more accurately, *the eating of* good food). It is good only because it causes a pleasant flavor sensation and/or because it promotes good health (depending on whether you are a connoisseur or a health nut). Even the healthfulness that results from a wholesome diet is only instrumentally good. We don't desire health for its own sake but in order to be free from the discomfort of illness and to be able to engage in the activities that we enjoy, such as bike riding, swimming, playing basketball, or just being able to walk around and live independent of others. It is hard to imagine having good health and yet not being able to do any of these things. Perhaps we can think of Endymion from Greek mythos. According to the story, he was a mortal man who was beloved by the moon goddess, Celene. She could not bear the thought of him growing old and dying so she cast a spell on him to stop his aging. Unfortunately, as a side effect, the spell made him sleep 24/7. Endymion had better health than any mortal; he did not even grow old! But what good was it for him? He could not enjoy his own health because he was in a state of permanent unconsciousness. It would not be any worse for him if he were a sickly invalid. His health gave him no benefit, so it was not good. For most of us, however, health provides benefits (or helps us avoid harms) and so is instrumentally good.

According to utilitarianism, when we calculate the total good and bad consequences resulting from an action, we must consult only the *intrinsically* good and bad consequences. Otherwise, if we counted both intrinsically and instrumentally good and bad consequences, then one action might be considered better than another action merely because it ultimately leads to the same good consequences by a more circuitous route. But instrumentally good things have their goodness only from the good things they help to bring about. (If my money fails to buy me or anyone else happiness and only causes trouble, then my money is not even instrumentally good.)

The question now is what sorts of things are intrinsically good? Here are three plausible candidates: moral virtue, knowledge (or wisdom), and happiness. After all, don't people often say, "Virtue is its own reward"? And don't we generally praise the pursuit of "knowledge for its own sake"? There is a problem, however, with positing multiple kinds of intrinsic goods. If we are to do the action that leads to the best overall consequences, then what do we do if one action does more to cultivate virtue in the world while another action does more to increase human knowledge? There is no way of saying how much one of these goods is worth how much of another. The goods of virtue, knowledge, and happiness are *incommensurable*.

For this reason it would be much easier if we could reduce right and wrong to one kind of intrinsic good. Traditionally, utilitarians have held that only happiness is intrinsically good, and only pain is intrinsically bad. Virtue and knowledge are only instrumentally good, and vice and ignorance are only instrumentally bad. While it may not be obvious that virtue and knowledge are *only* instrumentally good, it is undeniable that they are (usually) instrumentally good. Virtues like charity help to spread joy, while virtues like compassion help to eliminate suffering. Virtuous acts definitely help to make the world a better place overall. Knowledge also typically promotes happiness and prevents pain. Biological knowledge, for example, has helped to eliminate crippling diseases, such as polio and smallpox. Agricultural knowledge has helped to prevent starvation. Happiness, however, is never instrumentally good. It is only intrinsically good. Happiness is good not because of something else that it helps us to attain; it is good only for its own sake. For those reasons, most utilitarians claim that all happiness, and only happiness, is intrinsically good; and all pain, and only pain, is intrinsically bad.

According to the standard form of utilitarianism, the right action is the one that maximizes happiness and/or minimizes pain for everyone concerned. Though philosophers debate what exactly constitutes happiness, these discussions tend to get rather esoteric, and so we need not concern ourselves with that question. We just need to keep in mind that the concept of "happiness" includes (or is constituted by) many things: physical or sensual pleasure, intellectual pleasure, the realizations of one's hopes and aspirations, and so on. Likewise, pain or suffering can include physical pain, emotional pain, disappointment, or the frustration of one's desires.

UTILITARIANISM AND INDIVIDUAL ABORTIONS

Let us first look at how utilitarianism applies to the question of whether it is morally wrong to have an abortion, and put aside, for now, the question of whether it is morally wrong to allow people to have abortions (i.e., whether it should be legal). According to utilitarianism, abortion would be morally acceptable if and only if having an abortion resulted in as much or more happiness compared to the alternative of carrying the fetus to term (and then either raising the baby or giving it up for adoption).

So how does abortion affect the happiness and unhappiness of the various parties involved? Well, that is quite impossible to tell. Abortion will have very different consequences to different people in different situations. Consider the situation of an impoverished and mentally disabled woman with an ectopic pregnancy (in which the fetus is implanted in the fallopian tubes). Having an abortion would clearly have much better consequences for her than not having an abortion. Never mind about her poverty or disability; without the abortion she will die along with the fetus. Now contrast that with a wealthy, married woman in good health who wants to have children. In her case, having an abortion would have much worse consequences than carrying it to term. (Of course, she probably would not choose to have an abortion if she wanted children, but whatever.)

The standard version of utilitarianism determines the rightness or wrongness of each particular action on a case-by-case basis. Approaching the issue this way, we cannot say whether abortion is right or wrong; we can only say whether some *particular* abortion (e.g., Jane Smith aborting her fetus on December 18, 2008) is right or wrong.

This means that utilitarianism is highly context-dependent. An action in one particular set of circumstances could be morally wrong, while the same action, in slightly different circumstances, could be morally right. Let's go back to the example of my friend and her unfortunate cooking. Which course of action would maximize overall happiness will depend greatly on the particular details of the situation. If my friend is hypersensitive and insecure (and sufficiently gullible), then I have reasons to lie to her. But if she is thick-skinned, or if she would be more hurt by being deceived and is likely to see through my lies, then I have good reasons to tell her the truth.

Of course, it is often not possible to know enough of these details to determine what course of action would have the best consequences. I might, for example, tell my friend that her cooking is delicious, expecting to make her feel good, and she might surprise me by replying, "Really?! I think it is awful. Here, you can have the rest of mine!" Utilitarians get around this problem by positing rules of thumb. When you are unsure of what action would have the best consequences you should go with what *usually* works. Lying, stealing, killing, and so on almost always have worse consequences than the alternatives. So, generally, you should avoid these sorts of activities. But these are just approximate guides, shortcuts that we use to figure out what will probably be the best thing to do. If you know, or have good reason to believe, that breaking one of these rules will have better consequences than keeping it, then you should ignore the rule. I know that lying to the Nazis would have the best consequences, so that is my duty, even though lying is wrong in most ordinary contexts.

Whether an abortion is morally right or wrong, according to act-utilitarianism, will depend greatly on the particular details of the circumstances.

Since we do not have the space in this book to consider the particular details surrounding every woman who has ever wanted to have an abortion, it might be more productive for us to try to formulate a rule of thumb, based on the *typical* consequences, while keeping in mind that there will be exceptions to the rule whenever breaking it would have better consequences than following it.

To determine a rule of thumb about the rightness and wrongness of abortion we must consider the typical consequences of abortion, and compare those to the typical consequences of the alternatives. The typical situation that is relevant to the abortion issue will be an unwanted pregnancy, since people who want children usually do not consider having an abortion. For this typical situation we will also assume that the pregnancy does not significantly threaten the health of the mother, that the fetus does not suffer from severe birth defects or congenital illness, and that the pregnant woman is not in an environment that is wholly unsuitable for safely carrying to term and raising a child (such as a refugee camp). Extraordinary circumstances such as these make for obvious exceptions to any general rule. Even reasonable people on the pro-life side might grant that abortion is acceptable in these situations.

So what are the consequences of terminating a normal, unwanted pregnancy? And what are the consequences of the alternatives (carrying the fetus to term and either raising it or giving it up for adoption)?

CONSEQUENCES TO THE FETUS AND THE FUTURE PERSON

First let us look at the consequences to the fetus—not to the future person that the fetus would become if allowed to develop (that will come later), but only to the fetus itself. I think it is safe to say that the only good or bad things that could conceivably happen to a fetus are pleasure and pain. A fetus cannot feel fear or embarrassment, and it has no hopes or dreams to be frustrated. It has no desires and so cannot be disappointed. It has no beliefs, so it cannot be deceived.

The abortion procedure is undeniably gruesome, and pro-life propaganda devices such as the short film *Silent Scream* horrify audiences with the thoughts of fetuses painfully torn asunder. But at what point can a fetus feel pain? Certainly a zygote, which is merely a fertilized egg cell, cannot feel pain. Nor is it conceivable that an early embryo can feel pain, since its cells have not yet specialized into different types of cells, let alone distinct organs. Our best scientific evidence indicates that a living organism needs to have nerve cells hooked up in a certain way for it to be able to feel anything. The zygote and the early embryo have no neurons whatsoever, and so cannot experience anything at all. On the other hand, it seems obvious that a nine-month-old fetus can feel pain. So when exactly does the fetus acquire the capacity to feel? This is a scientific question. Virtually all experts (neurophysiologists, biologists, and medical researchers) agree that the fetus cannot feel pain before twenty weeks, and recent studies indicate that it might even be as late as twenty-nine weeks. On the other hand, even if the fetus could feel pain, this could be avoided simply by the use of anesthesia.

So as long as the abortion is performed early enough, or anesthesia is used, there is no pain to the aborted fetus. But utilitarianism demands that we do what would have the best overall consequences, not just the best immediate, short-term consequences. Thus we must consider what are the consequences of an abortion to the future person that the fetus would become if allowed to develop normally, not just to the fetus itself here and now. If the fetus is aborted, then that future person will not exist, and so will not enjoy any good consequences nor suffer any bad consequences. There will be no happiness and no sorrow, nothing to go in the plus column and nothing to go in the minus column—zero.

Now we must compare this to the alternative of carrying the fetus to term, after which it will develop and have a complete human life, barring some unfortunate accident. If this life that the fetus would grow up to live were to have more suffering than joy, then it would be a better thing if this person were not allowed to exist. (This person's life would add more to the negative column than to the positive column, meaning that the overall happiness in the universe would be lower with this person in it.) That would provide some justification for the woman to have an abortion. It is not enough to show that it would be right to have an abortion, because utilitarianism requires that we maximize happiness for everyone. For all we know, this future person might bring an abundance of happiness to a great number of other people, even though his own life is disappointing to him. Knowing only that the life the fetus would live, if given the chance, would be overall unhappy, the balance of reasons *so far* favors having an abortion. If everything else were more or less the same whether the fetus were to be aborted or not, then it would be OK to abort the fetus in this case.

Since we are looking for moral rules of thumb, we are considering only the typical, ordinary case. We are setting aside cases of severe birth defects or intolerable living conditions. The question, then, is whether the typical person in our society experiences more happiness than pain in a lifetime. Despite the fact that most people seem to complain a lot more than they celebrate, there is good reason to believe that most people are, on balance, significantly happy. Most people have a strong aversion to premature death and a strong desire to live out the entirety of their natural life span (or at least they do before they become old and infirm). If your continued life promised more bad than good, you would probably not be very enthusiastic about continuing it as long as possible. No doubt, some people perceive their lives to have more pain than happiness, especially those who are severely ill or injured. And it might be rational for them to prefer to die. But most of us have a decided preference to continue living, and if the fetus grows up to be a typical person in average circumstances, then it will share this preference. Thus we can assume that the future person who the fetus will become will experience much more happiness than unhappiness.

The probable overall happiness of the person the fetus will become provides some support for a general rule against abortion. One major problem with this sort of argument, however, is that it also provides some support for certain people not to practice contraception, or even abstinence. If we count the happiness of future people who may or may not exist, then some people will have a duty to have kids, even if they prefer not to. I will use myself as an example. I am in a steady, monogamous relationship. I have a steady job with good pay and great security. Furthermore, this job allows me lots of flexibility and a great deal of free time (depending on how ambitious I am). I am also a very reliable and responsible person with an even temperament and a very patient disposition. Given all that, there is good reason to think that any children I had would grow up to lead very happy lives. They would be raised in a big house with well-educated parents who love each other. They would have all of the opportunities necessary for success in life.

The fact is, however, that I do not want to have kids. I have never been one to get all mushy when I see a baby. (It is a different story with cats and dogs.) I prefer to devote most of my free time to furthering my philosophical career and enjoying my many hobbies. According to a utilitarian analysis, it would be wrong for me to use contraception, or even to abstain from sex (with my significant other). The happiness of whatever future children I would have would almost certainly outweigh the overall reduction to my happiness. (I never said I *hated* kids.) Maybe the utilitarian would say that I have a duty to have kids because it would increase the overall happiness of the universe (even though it would not increase the overall happiness of all of the *currently existing* people in the universe). But if you do not think that I have such a duty, then you must reject the utilitarian argument supporting that conclusion, either by rejecting utilitarianism altogether or by refusing to apply it to future people who might never exist. The utilitarian argument for my duty to have kids is the same argument as the utilitarian argument for a general rule against abortion. If you reject one, then you must reject the other.

CONSEQUENCES TO THE WOMAN HAVING THE ABORTION

One of the most popular arguments these days against abortion is that it is "bad for women." Pro-lifers claim that many women who have abortions later regret their choice. They cite studies indicating that women who terminate their pregnancies have high rates of depression, drug abuse, suicide attempts, and other mental illnesses. They refer to this cluster of negative side effects as "postabortion syndrome." Furthermore, they claim that abortion is a risky procedure performed at poor-quality facilities by unskilled technicians, with a high incident of injury. They argue that these bad consequences of abortion for the women who have them justify banning the procedure.

This argument is part of a strategy adopted by pro-life activist groups. Realizing that public opinion is against a complete ban on abortion, due to sympathies with the plight of those women who feel that they need to terminate their pregnancies, the pro-life groups decided they needed to undermine this sympathy. The bad-for-women argument is a tactic designed to hijack the strongest motivation for pro-choice attitudes in favor of keeping abortion legal. What is the merit of this bad-for-women argument?

First, let us assume for the sake of argument that these claims are correct, that abortion typically does have negative effects on the women who get one. Banning abortion on these grounds would be an example of *paternalism*. Paternalism refers to policies or laws that limit a person's freedom for his or her own good. Examples of paternalism would include laws requiring drivers to wear seatbelts, antidrug laws, and laws against committing suicide. If I choose to ride a motorcycle without a helmet or smoke crack in the privacy of my own home, I am only hurting myself. Thus, laws against these activities are aimed at protecting me from my own poor decisions.

Are paternalistic laws morally justifiable? Many philosophers, including J. S. Mill (the most famous utilitarian), have argued against paternalism on the grounds that the individual usually knows better than anyone else what is best for himself. Maybe I would be better off if I smoked crack occasionally. That seems unlikely, but I am in a better position to make that judgment than the state, my boss, or my family. Maybe I do not really value sobriety as much as most people do. But these arguments against paternalism are not entirely convincing. Most people who smoke crack are less happy than they would be if they were clean. Most people who refuse to don their seatbelt come to regret that decision when they are involved in a serious automobile collision.

On the other hand, there are many activities that people engage in that are risky or potentially detrimental to their health. Mountain climbers and hang gliders risk injuries that are easily as bad, and much more likely, than the injuries that occur to those who do not wear seatbelts. Even relatively safer pursuits, such as skiing and scuba diving, involve unnecessary risks to life and limb. Should we outlaw all of these activities in order to protect those who engage in them? Part of the reason we do not ban mountain climbing, hang gliding, and base-jumping is that people who engage in these sorts of activities consider them to be an important part of their lives, something that largely defines their personal identity. This is not generally so with people who refuse to wear seatbelts. Scuba diving is not just something I do for fun; it is part of what makes me the person I am. (My scuba instructor even described himself as having "devoted his life to aquatics," as if it were some sort of religious calling.) Obviously the decision to have a child or not (even if one gives it up for adoption) is an important part of one's life and personal identity. It is more like the decision to become a mountain climber or get a pilot's license than the decision not to wear a seatbelt or to ride a motorcycle without a helmet.

The pro-lifer, however, might point out that this appeal to personal identity and self-actualization does not refute paternalism according to a utilitarian analysis. If a mountain climber falls to his death, he very likely will rue the day that he took up his hobby. If (God forbid) I ever suffer from a lung expansion injury, I will probably curse my decision to become a certified diver. At any rate, it is plausible to think that I would be happier as a nondiving person without any major injury (and a little more money in my pocket) than I would be as a diver with a pulmonary embolism. After all, it is not as if there was something missing in my life before I took my first scuba class.

Maybe a utilitarian will have to concede that paternalism is often morally justified, even with regard to choices that we take to be largely definitive of our personal identities. The question then becomes whether abortion really is bad for women, as the pro-life argument claims. Does abortion generally cause a great deal of suffering to the women who get one? This is a factual claim, subject to evidence from observation. What do we find when we examine the observable evidence carefully? Abortion, like any other invasive medical procedure, has its risks. But carrying a fetus full term and giving birth is also accompanied by significant health risks. Pro-life and pro-choice activists present very different statistics to support their views. Each claims that the other's statistics are false or exaggerated. But if we go directly to a neutral source, such as the Centers for Disease Control, we find that pregnancy is significantly riskier than abortion. For example, from 1991 to 1997, the mortality rate from abortion procedure complications ranged between 0.3 and 0.6 deaths per 100,000. By comparison, the mortality rate from pregnancy complications for 1991 to 1999 was 9.6 deaths per 100,000 for women aged twenty to twenty-four. (Pregnancy is even riskier for women in older age groups.)

What about the other pro-life claim, that abortion causes depression and other mental health problems? The scientific evidence indicates that abortion poses little or no threat to mental health. In fact, the term "postabortion syndrome" has not been accepted by any major medical, psychiatric, or psychological organization. It is a term that has been invented by pro-life propagandists. A panel appointed by the American Medical Association concluded, from the vast body of studies on the issue, that first-trimester abortions pose no significant health hazards for most women. According to the panel, 76 percent of women who have an abortion report feeling relieved afterward. Although the rate of depression for women who have recently had abortions is 10 to 20 percent, that is the same rate of depression for all women of childbearing years—and lower in women who have recently given birth, as many women suffer from postpartum depression shortly after delivery. Ironically, the guilt and anxiety that some women feel after getting an abortion is often caused by the hostile antiabortion protesters accosting them as they enter the clinic.

CONSEQUENCES TO OTHERS

Along with the consequences of abortion to the pregnant woman and the fetus (and the future person the fetus will become) we must also consider the consequences to other people. This is much harder to discern. If we consider that the future person that the fetus would become will be a typical person (not a moral saint like Albert Schweitzer and not a villain like Ted Bundy), then it is not clear that the existence of this future person would significantly increase (or decrease) the happiness of others around him. Of course, if its parents wanted to have children, this future person would bring great joy to them and other family members. But, of course, people who want children are unlikely to consider abortion. If the child is given up for adoption, that will bring great happiness to the adopting couple who wants but cannot have children. Giving up your newborn for adoption, however, is not an easy thing to do. Pro-life advocates who throw this out as an alternative to abortion are being entirely unrealistic. Besides, according to a utilitarian analysis, some women might have a duty to try to get pregnant just so they can give their children up for adoption, since the inconvenience to these women would be small compared to the joy they would give to infertile couples. That seems *extremely* unrealistic.

What about other people besides the parents? Well, my girlfriend makes me happy, and my life is more worthwhile with her in it. But would I be less happy if she had never been born? It is impossible to tell. I might be dating someone else who would make me just as happy. Of course, this is not exactly something I would tell her on Valentine's Day. But we need to recognize that the concept of the "soul mate" is a ridiculous myth. The idea that there is one person out of the six billion people on Earth that you were meant to be with is wildly unlikely.

Finally, there is the surprising fact, briefly mentioned in chapter 6, that abortion seems to lower crime rates. The significant drop in crime in the late '90s is best explained by abortion becoming legal in the early '70s. It makes sense, since most abortions are sought by poor, uneducated, single women whose children are more likely than the rest of the population to commit crimes as adults. The evidence is quite striking. For one, the reduction in crime for each state is proportionate to the abortion rate in that state. Of course, the pro-lifer is going to underscore the creepiness of this argument. It strikes us as monstrous, like treating a headache with a guillotine. Still, we must consider all of the consequences of abortion, good and bad.

CONSEQUENCES OF ABORTION RULES OR POLICIES

Another variation of the utilitarian approach applies the happiness-maximization principle to rules rather than to particular actions. According to this method, we should compare the consequences, in terms of overall happiness, that would result from adopting various rules about abortion. This allows us to avoid having to conclude that some woman might have a duty to abort her fetus, even though she wants to keep it. We can formulate the rules in such a way that they *allow for*, but never *require*, abortions in certain cases.

One rule might be to allow any woman to have an abortion at any time for any reason. We will call this the "extremely permissive" rule. On the opposite extreme would be the "extremely restrictive" rule forbidding all abortions regardless of circumstances. In between the two extremes would be "moderately permissive" rules that would allow for abortion in most cases with some limits (e.g., only in the first trimester, etc.) and "moderately restrictive" rules that would ban abortion in most cases with some exceptions (e.g., when the pregnant woman's life is at risk, or in the case of rape, etc.). There are, of course, several different versions of the moderate rules, depending on what restrictions are placed or what exceptions are allowed. Few people advocate the extremely permissive or extremely restrictive rules. Since the acceptance of one of the extreme rules would probably not maximize happiness, we should ignore them and consider only the more moderate rules.

As formulated, these rules govern only the decision of the pregnant woman to terminate her pregnancy. If the acceptance of some sort of moderately restrictive rule would maximize happiness, and a woman terminates her pregnancy even though her situation does not fall under any of the exceptions of this rule, then she acts wrongly. That means that we should disapprove of her actions, counsel others not to do likewise, and so on. But this says nothing about whether abortion should be allowed. To decide that, we need to determine what the consequences would be of the general acceptance of a rule requiring people to prevent others from getting abortions and compare that to the consequences of a rule requiring people to allow others to get abortions. To decide whether abortion should be legal, we need to consider the consequences, in terms of overall happiness, of criminalizing abortion and punishing either the women who get abortions and/or the doctors who perform them.

To make this clear, let us consider the case of adultery. On the rule-based utilitarian approach, adultery is wrong because if our society adopted a rule allowing people to cheat on their spouses, it would have much worse consequences than the rule forbidding extramarital affairs. But even though adultery is morally wrong, it would be wrong to outlaw adultery. Incarceration of adulterers, who pose no threat to society, would cause even more harm to the family. So adultery is morally wrong, but it would also be wrong to outlaw adultery.

CONSEQUENCES OF ALLOWING OR BANNING ABORTIONS

Whether or not abortion should be allowed is, for the utilitarian, a separate issue from the question of whether or not abortion is morally wrong. To make something illegal is to institute some sort of sanction against it. And the only justification for any action—including punishing someone—is that performing it (or accepting a general rule allowing it to be performed) would result in better consequences than not performing it (or accepting a general rule forbidding it). It does not matter, on this view, whether or not the person "deserves" to be punished—though obviously punishing the innocent and letting the guilty off the hook would almost always have disastrous consequences.

So whether or not abortion should be illegal, according to the utilitarian analysis, depends entirely on the consequences of making and enforcing laws banning abortion. Of course, if an act is wrong, then its wrongness might be related to whether or not it should be punished. Stealing is wrong because it usually has very bad consequences, and if outlawing it would result in fewer robberies, then outlawing it would probably have better consequences than not. But we would still have to weigh the good consequences of discouraging stealing against the other consequences of enforcing the law.

One consequence of banning abortion might be a reduction in the number of abortions. Whether this would be a positive or negative consequence, however, is a question that we have already found to have an ambiguous answer. One problem is that it is unclear whether we should (or even could) include the overall happiness of the future person that the fetus would become. If so, then it seems that we should also outlaw contraception and even abstinence—at least for wealthy, young, childless couples. That would be absurd. Also, we would have to consider the possibility that a woman who has an abortion now, while she is not fully ready for parenthood, might later have happier children down the line (children who would not exist if she were to keep this fetus now).

What about the consequences of banning abortions? Presumably, a legal ban on abortions would involve some sort of punishment for those who obtain and/or provide abortions. From a utilitarian perspective, considering only the results, the purpose of punishment is to prevent the undesirable behavior from occurring—either by deterring others, reforming the offender, or by rendering the offender unable to repeat the offence (e.g., through execution or incarceration).

First let us consider the consequences of punishing the woman who aborts her fetus. Certainly that will result in less happiness for her. That is true of every punishment. It would not be very effective punishment if did not diminish the happiness of the person punished. Since punishment by its very nature must cause unhappiness, there must be enough other good consequences of the punishing to outweigh the unhappiness caused to the person punished for the punishing to be morally justifiable. What would be the good consequences, if any, of punishing the woman? It is not obvious how punishment could reform her, or even what change in her personality is needed. The woman who terminates her pregnancy is not a threat to society, so we do not need to mold her character or keep her off the streets like we do with muggers, child molesters, or serial rapists. Of course, the pro-lifer should object that the woman is a threat to her own fetuses. A pro-choicer might respond that the fetus is not a "member of society," but that is just a technicality. If a serial killer preys only on hermits we should still punish him. These hermits may not be members of society, but they are still people and so deserve protection. This gets us back to the thorny question of whether the fetus has rights or deserves protection—an issue that we have examined in earlier chapters and found very hard to settle. But even if we think that the fetus should be protected, it does not seem that the woman who has terminated her pregnancy is a threat to anyone. It is not as if she is going to run out and get pregnant again just so that she can have another abortion.

What if we assume that abortion is bad thing and needs to be prevented? Will punishing the woman, or the doctor, serve as deterrence and prevent future abortions? Most doctors would probably be deterred merely by the loss of their license to practice. The typical doctor has invested much of her life to training in pursuit of a medical career. And most doctors are paid very well. Thus most doctors will feel that they have too much to lose and will not be likely to risk the right to practice their vocation.

"BACK-ALLEY" ARGUMENT

It is common sense to think that punishing doctors would make them much less willing to perform abortions. But would criminalizing abortion actually reduce the number of abortions performed? A popular argument among pro-choice advocates is to claim that a ban on abortion would only lead to an increasing number of unsafe "back-alley" abortions, which would ultimately result in a great number of injuries and deaths to desperate women seeking to terminate their unwanted pregnancies. They reason that outlawing the abortion procedure would discourage doctors and legitimate healthcare institutions from providing abortion services, but it would do nothing to reduce the demand. Eventually, those who feel that they need an abortion will turn to the black market where unqualified abortionists, working in unsanitary conditions, would fill this need.

Those on the pro-life side might object that the back-alley argument is irrelevant because women who seek illegal abortions are guilty of making imprudent decisions. They have the choice to carry the fetus to term. The fetus, on the contrary, is an innocent victim. We should not protect those who make poor choices at the expense of those who have no say in the matter. There are, however, two problems with this response. First of all, we are considering the morality of abortion through a utilitarian lens. Utilitarianism bases the rightness and wrongness of an action or policy solely on the total amount of happiness and suffering that would result. It does not allow for considerations of who *deserves* what. Everyone counts equally; all that matters is how much happiness or unhappiness results. Of course, the pro-lifer is free to reject the utilitarian theory. But there is an even bigger problem with the pro-life response to the back-alley argument. The claim that we should not protect the woman from her own risky choices undermines the pro-life argument that abortion is "bad for women." The pro-lifers cannot have it both ways. Either we should not protect people from their own bad choices (and thus we should allow women to get abortions even if doing so were bad for them), or we should protect people from their own bad choices (and thus we should do what is necessary to prevent women from choosing unsafe, illegal abortions). If allowing safe abortions would do a better of job of protecting the health of women than would criminalizing the procedure, then the paternalistic approach would favor legalization of abortion.

According to a utilitarian analysis, if banning abortion would lead to increased injury and death due to unsafe back-alley abortions, then that counts against a ban on abortion. There is much debate, however, as to whether or not criminalizing abortion would actually lead to large numbers of dangerous, back-alley procedures. Pro-choicers say it would, while pro-lifers express doubt. Reliable information on the prevalence of black market abortions is not easy to find. Pro-life and pro-choice advocates present strongly conflicting statistics. It is hard to know which side to believe. Part of the problem is that those who provide illegal services rarely keep reliable records and never report their activities to any regulatory agencies. Just as drug pushers do not report their profits to the IRS or their sales to the FDA, illegal abortion providers are not going to provide data to the Centers for Disease Control or charge their services to the woman's health insurance.

To properly assess the back-alley argument we need to find evidence from a neutral, apolitical, and reliable source. Even then, there is some inevitable guesswork involved. I obtained my information from the World Health Organization. According to their data, legal restrictions on abortion do not seem to affect the incidence of the procedure. In fact, the lowest rates of abortion are in western and northern Europe, where abortion laws are lax and abortion services are easily accessible. Furthermore, and not surprisingly, where abortion is legal it is generally safe, and where abortion is unsafe it is typically not legal (or it is difficult to obtain). South Africa, to take just one example, legalized abortion in 1996, and the incidence of infection caused by abortion dropped by 52 percent. Taking all of this information into account, it seems that criminalizing abortion probably would not greatly reduce the numbers of abortions but would only increase the incidence of injuries from unsafe, illegal abortions. Judging from this data, the back-alley argument seems at least plausible.

CONCLUSIONS?

The consequences of abortion are a very complex matter. The overall outcomes resulting from individual abortions or from permissive or restrictive abortion policies are numerous. There is also the very difficult question of whether we should count consequences to people who might never exist. And some of the implications of this utilitarian analysis are very counter-intuitive. Therefore, we cannot say with any certainty whether abortion is right or wrong according to the utilitarian theory. Looking carefully at all of the facts, I have a hunch. But I will let the readers make their own calculations. On other hand, because of the vast complexity involved, perhaps utilitarianism is not the most useful theory for the issue of abortion.

SUGGESTED FURTHER READING

Bazelon, Emily. "Is There a Post-Abortion Syndrome?" *New York Times Magazine*, January 21, 2007, cover story.

Grady, Denise. "Study Finds 29-Week Fetuses Probably Feel No Pain and No Abortion Anesthesia." *New York Times*, August 24, 2005.

Messer, Ellen, and Kathryn May. *Back Rooms: Voices from the Illegal Abortion Era.* Amherst, NY: Prometheus Books, 1994.

Paul, Annie Murphy. "The First Ache." *New York Times Magazine*, February 10, 2008.

CHAPTER 10
VIRTUE

So far in this book we have been considering only the question of whether abortion is right or wrong or whether it is right or wrong to allow for abortions (i.e., whether it should be legal). This is to be expected, since the pro-life/pro-choice debate generally takes place on that battlefield. There is, however, another very different approach to moral questions that looks less at the rightness and wrongness of actions and more at the character of individuals committing the acts. This character-based approach to ethics is referred to as *virtue ethics*.

The first Western philosophers who ever made an extensive critical inquiry into questions of morality—philosophers such as Plato and Aristotle—formulated their theories in terms of character, virtue, and the good life rather than rules, consequences, or rights. Though virtue ethics lost much of its popularity among professional philosophers in the late Middle Ages, it has made a strong comeback in the past fifty years or so. Before we come to a conclusion on the issue of abortion, it is worth analyzing briefly the morality of abortion from the point of view of virtue ethics. Instead of concentrating solely on the rightness and wrongness of the act of intentionally terminating a pregnancy, we should ask how our attitudes about abortion reflect on our character. How would a morally good person think about abortion? As a mere trifle, as a serious crime, or as an unfortunate necessity?

VIRTUE ETHICS

The primary question of virtue ethics is not "What sorts of action should I do?" but rather "What sort of person should I be?" Its first concern is with a person's character, not with how a person's actions accord with some rule or procedure. So what is character? Let us start by asking a more commonsense question. If you want to judge what sort of person I am or what my character is like, what would you look at? One obvious answer is that you would look at my actions, at what sorts of things I do. If I keep my promises, then I am honest; if I share with others, then I am generous; and so on. This is still about actions, so what makes the virtue ethics approach different? First of all, looking at particular actions is not enough to discern a person's character. Suppose I keep a promise on one occasion. Does that mean that I am an honest man? Hardly. Honesty does not consist of keeping a promise or telling the truth on one occasion. The honest person keeps his word all (or almost all) of the time. Character is not constituted by particular actions but by a *pattern* of actions over a course of time, and ultimately over a lifetime.

There is still more to character than just behavior, even when it is looked at as a general pattern of conduct. What if I always keep my word, but I do so only because I am sure that I would get caught if I lied, and I worry that no one would trust me anymore? Maybe I would lie, cheat, and break my promises if I ever thought that I could get away with it. In that case I might be better than those who *do* lie and cheat with no fear of getting caught, but not by much. I would not be a truly honest man even though I never actually *do* anything dishonest. Virtue, then, involves more than just actions. What motivates us to act—the feelings, beliefs, and values that move us to act the way that we do—is also important. Virtuous people have the proper attitudes and good values. They have the right priorities. One who gives to the poor out of sympathy is generous and compassionate. One who gives to the poor only to gain the admiration of others is not generous but merely vain and self-absorbed (and probably insincere to boot). Of course, we should still praise the vain person's *act* of charity, but we should not praise the person's *character*, and we should not offer him up as a role model.

Of course, the virtue ethicist does not deny that certain actions are morally right and certain actions are wrong. But right and wrong are thought of as derivative concepts. For an action to be morally right means that it is the kind of action that the virtuous person would do (in those sorts of circumstances); morally wrong actions are the sorts that vicious people would do. This is given more specific detail by describing the particular features of a morally good person. A good person is one who is true to his word, is generous with his time and money, and feels sympathy with those less fortunate.

What determines which personal traits are virtues and which are vices? Traditionally, virtue ethicists have claimed that a certain conception of the good life constitutes what is objectively good for human beings. Developing and exercising certain traits and adopting a certain sort of lifestyle constitute what is well-being for a normal human person, even if that person does not desire to have those traits and gets no pleasure from exercising them. There are certain values that we should have, certain activities that we should pursue—not because of any subjective preference, but because these would make for an objectively better human life. This notion of the good life is analogous to health. Although most people feel better overall when they are healthy, not everything that feels good is good for you. (The most delicious food, for example, is usually not the most wholesome.) Furthermore, it is an objective fact that certain activities promote health while others threaten it. Exercise and a low-fat diet lead to good health. And good health can be objectively measured by features such as proportionate height to weight, moderate blood pressure, and good muscle tone. It is not merely a matter of opinion or subjective feeling of satisfaction. It is similar with the good life. A certain lifestyle of well-rounded experiences, moderation in work and pleasure, and mutually affectionate, deep personal relations constitute what is an objectively good life and is more worthy of pursuit than other lifestyles, such as the money-obsessed work addict or the hedonistic playboy.

The highest aim of human life is not *happiness*, at least not in the ordinary sense of some subjective state of pleasure or contentment. Instead the goal of a human life is to *thrive* or to *flourish*, which means (in part) to fully realize certain capacities that are partly definitive of what it is to be a human being, such as developing one's talents, making and maintaining friendships, and dealing honestly and fairly with others. Certain sorts of lives are more worth living, not because they bring more subjective feelings of satisfaction but because they fulfill our human nature more completely.

VIRTUE ETHICS, ABORTION, AND PARENTHOOD

Virtue ethics does not easily allow for a definitive conclusion on the rightness or wrongness of abortion. We cannot look only at the action; we must also look at the motives. A woman who regretfully terminates her fetus that has been diagnosed with Tay-Sachs (a disease that will cause the baby to die before its third birthday) because she wants to prevent the pointless suffering of her innocent child, with no thought to her own inconvenience, demonstrates compassion and could not reasonably be denounced as callous or selfish. On the other hand, another woman in a similar situation who obtains an abortion merely because she does not want stretch marks, and who uses the fact that her fetus has Tay-Sachs as a convenient excuse to avoid the criticism of others, is vain and selfish, even if we think she is ultimately doing the right thing. She is acting for the wrong sorts of reasons. Virtue ethics, in this way, is more about our values and attitudes than it is about our actions.

Virtue ethics has even less to say about whether abortion should be legal. This is because the law cannot dictate how we should feel or think, only what we should do. A common cliché heard all too often says, "You cannot legislate morality." In one sense this is clearly false; we outlaw stealing, murder, rape, and fraud at least in part because they are morally wrong. But while we can legislate moral *behavior*, we cannot legislate moral *character*. We could outlaw abortion, but we cannot legally require people to feel reverence for human life. We cannot make it a law that people must value parenthood for its own sake.

Not too long ago, a philosopher named Rosalind Hursthouse applied virtue ethics to the issue of abortion. Rather than pondering the moral status of the fetus or the rights of pregnant women (both of which are better saved for debates about whether abortion should be legal), she looked at how our abortion attitudes reflect upon our character. What sorts of values are revealed in a person's response to abortion, and are these values consistent with what is naturally, intrinsically good for human beings?

From the virtue ethics perspective, we cannot make blanket statements about abortion. We cannot say that every woman who terminates her pregnancy is thereby a bad person or that every woman who terminates her pregnancy is blameless. Much depends on the reasons behind the decision. Nevertheless, Hursthouse's position ultimately leans slightly to the pro-life side. She argues that a strongly pro-choice attitude not only fails to appropriately respect the life of the fetus, but also fails to recognize that raising children is an important part of the good life for most people, part of what constitutes "flourishing" for most typical human beings. Of course, she recognizes that some people will be unfit parents (although being unfit to raise kids is inconsistent with being virtuous) and that some people will lack the means to adequately care for children (although those people could hardly be said to be *flourishing*).

More important, there is no vice in forgoing parenthood in order to pursue some other important and worthy goal. Albert Schweitzer and Mother Teresa could not have dedicated their lives to the poor with a brood of youngsters in tow. We would not say that either of them lacked virtue simply because they did not have kids. On the contrary, they are typically held up as moral exemplars. Nevertheless, if parenthood is part of the good life, then a virtuous person like Albert Schweitzer would see forgoing child rearing as some sort of sacrifice that he had to make for the good of others.

One who sees child rearing primarily as a burden to be avoided has, to that extent, skewed values and a deep character flaw. And on this view, forgoing parenthood to avoid the responsibility of childcare and to continue to enjoy a carefree existence is immature and irresponsible.

According to Hursthouse, for those who have adequate conditions in place to become decent parents without excessive burden—conditions such as a loving partner, a stable income, and a healthy environment—raising children is part of a complete life. Raising productive members of the next generation is something we should all do, not as a burdensome duty or as the necessary means for furthering the good of society, but as something to be valued for its own sake. Of course, properly valuing parenthood is not a decisive factor in determining whether it is right or wrong to have an abortion on a particular occasion, and it says little or nothing about whether abortion should be legal. But it does tell us what the morally good person would think and do, and so gives indirect indication of what sorts of actions are morally right or wrong.

One problem with this narrow conception of the good life is that it focuses on bad reasons for avoiding parenthood but does not address all of the bad reasons for which people have children. Many people have children for selfish reasons. Some people are lonely and want to receive love from their children (rather than wanting to give love to their children). Some people who feel that they have not accomplished what they wanted to in life try to live vicariously through their children's accomplishments. Some people want children to take over a family business or just want to be taken care of when they grow old and infirm. All of these are selfish reasons, but I think that many people who have children for these reasons can still be good parents. In fact, it is hard to see how one could decide to have children for reasons that were not at least partly selfish. It is hard to be motivated to have children solely for the sake of the children themselves, because those children do not exist yet. I can be motivated to take home a stray dog for the dog's sake—but that is because the dog exists, and I can look into its sad puppy eyes and be moved to kindness. Maybe it is possible to do that with a late-stage fetus if we see it on an ultrasound, but it is harder to be motivated to try to get pregnant for the sake of the future offspring who would not otherwise exist.

A bigger problem with this view is that is seems to make contraception wrong, at least in some cases. Avoiding pregnancy is not necessarily wrong, even if parenthood is part of the good life. For one, there are many components to the good life, and one might not be able to fit all of them into a human life of normal duration. So one can, on this view, still live a good life without raising children as long as one engages in enough of the other pursuits that make life worthwhile. But "having a good time" is not considered important enough to forgo the goods of parenthood, and those who avoid pregnancy simply in order to have more fun in life are irresponsible people.

Second, insofar as this view does imply that using contraception is morally objectionable when it is done only to continue enjoying a carefree life without the burden of kids, it does not imply that using contraception is *as* shameful as getting an abortion. Hursthouse claims that the strongly pro-choice attitude manifests not only a lack of proper appreciation for the importance of parenthood but also a lack of respect for the life of the fetus. Just how much respect the fetus is due depends largely on how fully developed it is. An eight-month-old fetus is more fully developed, and thus more human, than a one-month-old embryo. Just as it is natural to mourn the miscarriage at eight months more than the miscarriage at one month, we should also disapprove of late-term abortions more than we do early term abortions. The late-term fetus is due more respect because it represents human life more than the relatively undeveloped embryo does.

Nevertheless, it seems odd to say that the use of contraception is in *any* way irresponsible or morally objectionable. What is so bad about wanting to have a good time? Perhaps one reason we tend to think that someone who lives life with the primary aim of having the most fun possible is irresponsible is because we assume that such a person is neglecting his duties to others. We picture the prodigal son who spends his inheritance while neglecting his elderly parents. Or we imagine the party animal who gets sloppy drunk every night. But what about the enlightened hedonist who enjoys a simple life of moderation, who pursues a career doing something she enjoys, and who engages in her favorite hobbies in her free time? She is a productive member of society, pays her taxes, and takes care of her parents when they grow old. Is she a bad person just because she worries that having children will not allow her time for sailing, golf, and travel?

There is too much disagreement about exactly what constitutes the good life for us to use a particular conception of the good life in analyzing the morality of abortion. Catholics, for example, think that raising children is a crucial component of the good life (at least for laypeople). Buddhists, on the other hand, value nonattachment, while hedonists think that only pleasure is worth pursuing for its own sake. Perhaps some of these views are better than others, but it would require another book longer than this just to scratch the surface of that debate. It is unlikely that we will be able to settle the point here.

Perhaps we can still analyze our attitudes toward abortion in terms of specific virtues such as kindness and compassion, or of certain vices such as callousness and selfishness, without making claims about what sorts of things make life good and what should be the ultimate aim for all human life. We can start by looking at the various attitudes toward the fetus/embryo that are manifest in the pro-life and pro-choice attitudes.

CHARACTER AND RESPECT FOR LIFE

Let us start with the pro-choice attitude toward the fetus and how this might reflect on one's character. People who advocate a woman's right to choose have many reasons for doing so, and we must avoid overgeneralizing. So let us describe a particular pro-choice stance while keeping in mind that it does not describe all (or even most) of those who consider themselves to be pro-choice.

Some people with extreme pro-choice sentiments think that abortion is a bad thing only insofar as it is an inconvenience to the woman and an unpleasant experience for her. The fetus, on this view, has no moral consideration. How does this way of thinking about abortion reflect on the moral character of the radical pro-choicers who see it this way? Does it reflect some vice? Would a virtuous person see abortion in this way?

We must put aside whether or not we think the pro-choice view is correct. People can have decent moral views for deplorable reasons. For example, a man might be fully in favor of the legal and material equality of women only because he hopes that if such a state of affairs is realized, then he will "get laid" more often (i.e., because he is lascivious) or he will not have to pay for dinner when on a date (i.e., because he is cheap). Let us assume, for the sake of argument, that the pro-choice view about the rightness and wrongness of abortion is correct, that we have no moral duties to the fetus or the future person that it might become. Might there still be something wrong with one who refuses to see abortion as a moral matter of any significance?

Here is an example of how an action or attitude can reflect poor character even when there is no wrongdoing. I do not think that a human being has any moral obligations to an insect or a spider. Perhaps we have obligations not to eliminate certain species, but we have no duty to individual bugs. Bugs are not rational, thinking creatures and they cannot experience pleasure or pain. Thus they cannot be meaningfully said to have interests and cannot be harmed. Now suppose eight-year-old Sammy likes to torture insects by pulling off their legs one by one and watching them squirm. (It might not be real torture, since the bug cannot feel pain, but he is still enjoying the perceived or imagined pain of another creature.) I find the child's behavior morally repugnant, and I expect most people in our society would agree with me, not because we have sympathy for the insect, or because we believe that the bug has moral rights, but because of the cruel intentions of the child. If Sammy were my son, I would discourage the behavior—not because the act itself is wrong but because that sort of behavior makes Sammy a bad person. I would not lie to him and tell him that insects are persons like us. Instead I would try to cultivate within the boy a respect for all life. Part of my worry, of course, would be that little Sammy might move up to other animals, torturing mice, kittens, or even people. (Many serial killers tortured animals when they were young.) But even if there were no reason to think that Sammy will ever harm anything except insects, and even if he acknowledges that his victims have no conscious experience, he would be a better person if he did not indulge his cruelty, even in harmless ways.

We could say something similar about one's attitude toward the fetus. Even if it can feel no pleasure or pain, even if it cannot think, even if there were no reason for thinking it has any moral rights; still, there is something objectionable about those who are not disturbed by graphic descriptions of the abortion procedure or are morally indifferent to abortion, seeing it as no more problematic than getting a haircut or an appendectomy. These people have callous attitudes and lack sufficient respect for life.

Some antiabortion advocates have used the natural respect for life that most of us have as a powerful rhetorical device. They carry signs with gory pictures of aborted fetuses. Or they write essays describing a street littered with dead fetuses and then ask if we would callously step on them. But as effective as this is in motivating public opinion, it is not proof that abortion is wrong, that the fetus has rights, or that we should criminalize the procedure. What attitudes we have or should have is an important component of moral character. It may even be some indication that an action is right or wrong. If good people avoid acting that way and would disapprove of such actions in others, then that is a reason to think that the action is morally wrong. But if there are other reasons to think that there is nothing morally wrong with the action (for example, no one is harmed), then maybe moral character and right action can diverge. Maybe the good person can do the wrong thing for good reasons. (As they say, "the road to hell is paved with good intentions.") There is no reason to think that the attitudes that determine our character are infallible indicators of right and wrong.

Many pro-choice people, of course, do have at least some respect for life. Although they think that abortion should be legal and available to those who need it, they also think that it would be better if there were fewer abortions (or better yet, no abortions). They see abortion as an unfortunate necessity, which they would prefer to be less necessary. It is important to keep this in mind. Neither side has a monopoly on respect for life or on virtue generally. Though it may be true that a lack of respect for life is a vice more common to those on the pro-choice side, there are pro-lifers with so little respect for life that they bomb abortion clinics and assassinate doctors who work there.

ATTITUDES TOWARD THE PREGNANT WOMAN

We have considered one fairly extreme way of viewing abortion on the pro-choice side. Now we should look at an equally extreme viewpoint on the pro-life side and ask whether such a view manifests some character flaw.

Some on the pro-life side disapprove of abortion under any circumstances—even when pregnancy results from rape or when it threatens the health or life of the pregnant woman. Would a virtuous person hold such a view?

Just as certain radical pro-choice perspectives seem to involve a lack of respect for life, this view seems to involve a lack of respect for the pregnant woman. To view the fetus's rights and interests as outweighing the rights and interests of the pregnant woman is to view her as less than a person. Even to judge her rights and interests as roughly equal to that of the fetus involves the failure to recognize the woman as a rational, autonomous moral agent. The fetus is clearly not a person but only a potential person. To see the two as being on par is to treat the pregnant woman as if her only interest is to be biologically alive; it ignores the fact that she, unlike the fetus, is a rational, conscious subject, capable of having desires, making decisions, and having human emotions. Surely these are morally relevant characteristics, none of which are possessed by the fetus. Perhaps the fetus deserves some moral consideration for being *potentially* a person who *will* be capable of conscious experience, desires, and reason. But it should not be seen to deserve more, or even as much, moral consideration as an *actual* person. To grant such an elevated moral status to the fetus is to denigrate the moral status of the pregnant woman.

To think that the fetus's rights and interests outweigh those of the pregnant woman is to see her as little more than an incubator, a walking womb and not a person. And to ignore her rights and interests and allow her no choice in the matter is to treat her *merely as a means* (to borrow a phrase from the great eighteenth-century philosopher Immanuel Kant) to the development of the fetus and not as having any inherent value herself. A virtuous person would also feel at least a little sympathy toward those women whose misfortunes drive them to seek to terminate their pregnancy. To do otherwise would be even more callous than seeing the fetus as a mere tumor.

Thus, it seems that a virtuous person would not have either of these extreme attitudes on the abortion issue. Whether on the pro-life side or the pro-choice side, a virtuous person would have respect for the life of the fetus but also respect for the life *and* for the autonomy of the pregnant woman. A virtuous person would see abortion as something unfortunate, a symptom of social problems, and something that we should try to reduce. But a virtuous person would think that it would be better to reduce the *need* for abortion, by eliminating poverty and rape and by making contraception easily available, than to reduce the availability of abortion.

FANATICS

There is one personality flaw that is found on both sides of the pro-life/pro-choice debate: *self-righteousness*. Those who have entirely made up their mind on the issue and refuse even to consider the arguments supporting the opposing view manifest a particularly egregious moral flaw in their character. These fanatics have the arrogance to assume that they are smarter than, or morally superior to, anyone who disagrees with them, and they fail to show a minimal degree of respect for the opinions of others, whom they vilify as morally corrupt or dismiss as being ignorant or stupid. This vice can be found in the pro-life fanatics who assume that I must be a baby-killing monster just for considering arguments defending abortion and in the pro-choice fanatics who assume that I must be a woman-hating caveman for even entertaining the idea that abortion might be morally wrong.

A bit of self-righteousness might even be found in people like me who might think they are better than others because they carefully and critically weigh both sides of the issue while dismissing as "fanatics" those who feel more certain about the issue. Maybe I should have stayed at the pub and listened to the pro-lifers, described in the introduction, who accosted me.

Self-righteousness prohibits critical thinking and so is an obstacle to rational moral deliberation and to truth seeking. But according to virtue ethics, self-righteousness is not only instrumentally bad. The tendency to assume dogmatically that one is right and others are wrong—and that one is morally superior to his fellow human beings—is an inherently bad character trait. No wonder this human flaw is denounced above all others in the Gospels ("Let he who is without fault cast the first stone," "Judge not lest ye be judged," and, of course, the parable of the Pharisee and the tax collector.)

CONCLUSION

Having carefully examined the most common pro-life and pro-choice arguments, among both laypeople and professional philosophers, and having picked through these in some detail, now it is time for a conclusion. We may not be in a position for a final, once-and-for-all conclusion on whether abortion is morally wrong and should be banned or whether women have a right to terminate their pregnancy. We may not be able to end the debate for all time with unanimous agreement. The issue is so complicated that I could have made an entire book out of each chapter. And we philosophers are an inventive lot; I am sure that we will continue to come up with yet even more new arguments. But hopefully we can, at this point, be able to come at least to some preliminary conclusion that most of us can agree on.

What exactly this preliminary conclusion should be will have to be determined by the readers. As long as they judge the matter on the strength of the arguments alone and not on any irrational bias or emotional prejudice, they should all reach the same (or similar) final view. And as long as I was faithful to my goal of presenting both sides of the debate in a fair and accurate way, then that agreement should reflect what is really morally right or wrong about abortion. Unfortunately, we humans are finite and fallible. No reader is entirely unbiased, and no author entirely fair and even-handed. All I can hope is that my humble contribution to the issue can make some small improvement in the deliberation of some readers—or, failing that, at least I might cultivate an appreciation for the difficulty of the task and the need for careful, rational thinking about important moral matters.

SUGGESTED FURTHER READING

English, Jane. "Abortion and the Concept of a Person." *Canadian Journal of Philosophy* 5 (October 1974): 233–43.

Hursthouse, Rosalind. "Virtue Theory and Abortion." *Philosophy and Public Affairs* (1991): 223–46.

Maguire, Daniel C. "A Catholic Theologian at an Abortion Clinic." In *The Ethics of Abortion*, edited by Robert Baird and Stuart Rosenbaum, 199–206. Amherst, NY: Prometheus Books, 2001.

Selzer, Richard. "Abortion." In *The Ethics of Abortion*, edited by Robert Baird and Stuart Rosenbaum. Amherst, NY: Prometheus Books, 2001. (Selzer is the one who gives examples of streets littered with dead fetuses.)

Wolf, Naomi. "Our Bodies, Our Souls." *New Republic*, October 16, 1995.

INDEX

COUNTY COLLEGE OF MORRIS
LEARNING RESOURCE CENTER
214 CENTER GROVE ROAD
RANDOLPH, NEW JERSEY 07869